HOMILIES AGAINST
THE JEWS

HOMILIES AGAINST THE JEWS

John Chrysostom

Clemens & Blair, LLC

— 2025 —

CLEMENS & BLAIR, LLC

Clemens & Blair, LLC, is a non-profit educational publisher.
www.clemensandblair.com

Library of Congress Cataloging-in-Publication Data

Chrysostom, John (347-407 AD)
Homilies Against the Jews
A new English translation of: *Adversus Judaeos* (ca. 386 AD)

p. cm.
Includes bibliographical references

ISBN 978-1963-1431-64
(pbk.: alk. paper)

    1.   Christianity, history of
    2.   Jews, history of

Printing number: 9 8 7 6 5 4 3 2 1

Printed in the United States of America on acid-free paper.

ACKNOWLEDGMENT

The editor would like to thank O. G. for his extensive assistance in the preparation of this text.

CONTENTS

INTRODUCTION
THOMAS DALTON

John Chrysostom—later, Saint John, in the Catholic and Lutheran traditions—was born around the year 347 AD in the city of Antioch, which at that time was part of the Roman Empire (today, the city of Antakya, in south-central Turkey). As a young man, he studied the Greek language, became a lawyer, and eventually grew committed to Christianity. By his late 20s, he was practicing extreme asceticism in the attempt to both follow the 'way of Christ' and to demonstrate his heightened spiritual commitment. He memorized large portions of the Bible and extended his theological studies at the School of Antioch—one of the two main centers of Christian learning at that time (the other being Alexandria). In the year 381, Chrysostom became an ordained deacon, and by 388 he was an ordained presbyter (priest), at the age of just 41.

It was just around this time that he began to intensify his public speaking at Antioch's cathedral, giving impassioned liturgies and drawing large crowds; and in fact, 'Chrysostom' in Greek means 'golden-voiced' or 'golden-mouthed'—such was his reputation. His popularity grew rapidly over the next several years, until, in 397, at the age of 50, he was appointed archbishop of Constantinople, some 1,000 kilometers (650 miles) to the north of Antioch.

But all was not well. By the early 400s, he had alienated important rulers with his uncompromising brand of Christianity, and he was ultimately excommunicated and exiled. It was during one of his exilic journeys in 407 AD that he died at the age of 60.

Though he died young, Chrysostom left a large body of written work—over 1,000 distinct pieces, including sermons, letters, commentaries, and theological treatises. As a result of his immense learning and renowned popularity, he was soon named a saint, and would eventually become known as one of the most famous and influential Early (Greek) Church Fathers.

As it happens, and owing largely to its location at the very southern edge of modern-day Turkey, Antioch had a large Jewish population.

They had resided there at least since the 3rd century BC, but after the destruction of the Jewish temple in Jerusalem in 70 AD, large numbers of Jews were dispersed around the Middle East, and the population in Antioch grew significantly. By the mid-300s AD, there were large numbers of both Jews and Christians, and the two groups had many occasions to interact. It was in such a milieu that Chrysostom lived, and which caused him to react harshly against the Jewish influence.

We must recall that Jews have had a highly negative reputation in the West for centuries, even millennia.[1] As far back as 300 BC, we have critical remarks from philosophers, writers, and other notable figures; they complained about the Jews' "hatred of humanity," their inclination for animal (and human) sacrifice, their superstitious beliefs, their "exodus" as a group of diseased lepers, their tendency toward insurgency and revolution, their love of gold, and their general lack of good will toward others. And all this, prior to the Christian era.

With the coming of Christianity, there arose new complaints, primarily that Jews played a leading role in Jesus' crucifixion; the Jews "killed Christ," said some Christian zealots. Despite the "new way" of Jesus, Jews stubbornly clung to their old beliefs, rejecting the Savior and his followers. This led early Christian theologians to begin to write critically of the Jews: notably, Melito of Sardis, Tertullian, and Hippolytus of Rome all expressed critical views, roughly in the period 150 to 225 AD.

But things accelerated into the 4th century, when three major Christian Fathers adopted harshly anti-Jewish views: Gregory of Nyssa, Jerome of Stridon, and John Chrysostom. Thus it came to be that, in late summer of the year 386, Chrysostom crafted a series of eight sermons—"homilies"—attacking the Jews of his day. Of the three men, Chrysostom's homilies constitute the only extensive piece of writing that survives; in a very real sense, his lectures comprise the oldest existing "anti-Semitic" text in Western history.

*****

In order to better understand Chrysostom's critique, it will be helpful to review some basic events in the Jewish calendar. As he says early on

---

[1] See my book *Eternal Strangers* (2020) for a comprehensive study.

(I.1.5), the "festivals of the Jews are soon to march upon us".[2] He then cites by name the Feast of the Trumpets, the Feast of the Tabernacles, and "the fasts." To clarify, here are the annual events to which he refers, in roughly chronological order:

- Tisha B'av (July or August)
- Rosh Hashanah, aka "Feast of Trumpets" (late summer)
- Yom Kippur (autumn)
- Sukkot, aka "Feast of Tabernacles" (autumn)

Fasts are associated primarily with Tisha B'av and Yom Kippur, during which Jews abstain for 24 hours; there are also some half-dozen minor (12-hour) fasts throughout the year. But all four of these major events indeed come "in quick succession" each year, as Chrysostom says.

But the central question at hand is this: What, exactly, is Chrysostom's complaint? What reasons does he have for disliking the Jews? Unfortunately, we get no precise answer in the homilies. Rather, we find a series of charges, accusations, and complaints that are evidently based in daily experience and which have a long history; but Chrysostom does not take the time to elaborate. He seems to feel that his listeners have a good grasp of the many issues with the Jews and he thus has no real need to recount specific examples.

Still, it is worth reviewing here, at the outset, some of the charges and accusations that he levels against the Hebrews. The chief complaint, theologically speaking, is that one mentioned above: that the Jews "crucified Christ." This is a well-known and infamous claim, one that has caused countless problems for Jews over the centuries, and Chrysostom is one of the first to really press this point home.

For Christian readers, this is a major issue; but for the non-Christian, this holds no weight. Thus, of particular interest here are the *non-theological reasons* for disliking Jews. These are based not on the Bible but on real, tangible, concrete, and empirical claims against them— the types of issues that would concern anyone interacting with, or affected by, Jews. Especially in the present day, when many Jews are secular

---

[2] In the following citations, I will use a 3-digit designation, indicating Homily number, section, and paragraph. Thus, the cited passage appears in Homily I, section one, paragraph five.

or otherwise non-religious, Jews may yet retain many of the same negative characteristics that Chrysostom mentions—even if they can no longer be charged with the theological 'murder' of Jesus. These non-religious complaints are especially relevant today if, for example, modern-day critics cite the same or similar complaints; in which case, we can understand that today's critics are not just "mindless anti-Semites" but are recalling age-old complaints, ones which, owing to their persistence, are evidently grounded in biology and genetics.

Here, then, is a sampling of Chrysostom's non-religious accusations and complaints. Homily I includes the following assertions:

- Jews as "a disease" (I.1.5)
- Christians who are "sick with the Judaizing disease" (I.1.5)
- Jews as "pitiable and miserable" (I.2.1)
- Jewish "gluttony and drunkenness" (I.2.5)
- Equating "the theater and the synagogue" (I.2.7)
- Synagogue as "a brothel" (I.3.1)
- Synagogue as "a den of robbers and a lodging for wild beasts" (I.3.1)
- Jews' "hatred for mankind" (I.3.6)
- Jews frightening people "as if [they] were little children" (I.3.7)
- Jews who "live for their bellies," "gaping for the things of this world," no better than "pigs or goats," due to "their wanton ways and excessive gluttony" (I.4.1)
- Jews as deceivers, liars (I.6.4)
- Jews as "the infection of the whole world" (I.6.7)
- Jews' "plundering, covetousness, abandonment of the poor, theft, cheating in trade" (I.7.1)

And all this in Homily I! Though, to be fair, this first homily is, in many ways, the harshest; the remaining ones generally elaborate on themes laid out here in this initial sermon.

But let's take a moment to analyze this list of complaints. We have at least three "biological" slurs here in Homily I: Jews are a disease, an infection of the whole world; and those who might be tempted to follow the Jews are "sick with the Judaizing disease." This is precisely the kind of language that Hitler and his men were so condemned for, and yet, this was a very old complaint; in fact, we can go all the way back to the year 41 AD, when Emperor Claudius declared the Jews to be "a general plague which infests the whole world".[3] So even Chrysostom's language here is not unprecedented; such talk was at least 300 years old already in his day. ("Judaizing" Christians, incidentally, refers to Christians who either believe that the Old Testament laws are still binding on Christians, or who simply are attracted to, and fraternize with, Jews.)

Furthermore, we see here in Homily I that Jews are *vice-ridden*. Among their personal qualities are such things as gluttony, drunkenness, cruelty, prostitution, base materialism, and callousness toward the needy. They lie with impunity. Jews are portrayed here as morally deficient, as wanton, as profligates who live only for material and sensual pleasures. At the very least, they debase society, and at worst they set a negative example for the non-Jewish remainder of society, tempting others into their immoral ways.

Of special interest is the charge that Jews "hate mankind." This, again, is a very old accusation, dating back to Hecateus of Abdera in 300 BC, who wrote that the Jews were "to a certain extent misanthropic and hostile to foreigners".[4] Misanthropy, or hatred of all (non-Jewish) mankind, is a serious charge; what could motivate such a thing, apart from a collective psychopathology or mental illness? And yet, perhaps the single most persistent and most recurrent complaint against the Jews over the ages, is that of a hatred of mankind. It is as striking as it is telling.

Finally, Chrysostom asserts that the Jews are *outright criminals*; they steal, they cheat in business, they plunder. By such means, they simultaneously degrade society and enrich themselves. Those who would compete against the Jews are driven to the same lowly, illegal tactics. And when they manage to avoid punishment, they set yet another negative example; if the Jews can get away with crimes, why not everyone? As a result, they are indeed "pitiable and miserable," says John.

What else? A quick survey of the remaining homilies reveals such concerns as these:

---

[3] *Eternal Strangers*, p. 28.
[4] *Eternal Strangers*, p. 16.

- Jews act everywhere contrary to divine wishes (IV.4.2)
- Jews are "arrogant and obstinate" (V.4.4)
- Synagogues are "robber's dens and dwellings of demons" (V.12.12)
- "You give it [the synagogue] a name more worthy than it deserves if you call it a brothel, a stronghold of sin, a lodging-place for demons, a fortress of the devil, the destruction of the soul, the precipice and pit of all perdition" (VI.7.6)
- The Jews damage and destroy a person's very soul (VIII.3.10)
- By their "charms and spells," Jews claim to offer medical services and miracle cures (VIII.5.6)

For all this, Chrysostom is as quick to blame his fellow Christians as he is the Jews. Jews are obviously the root of the problem, but if non-Jews did not become "sick" and follow them, there would be little damage. And equally as bad are the many innocent bystanders: Christians who know someone who is sick with the "Judaizing disease" but do nothing to save their fellow man. Chrysostom is insistent: we must intervene, we must risk our own well-being, in order to keep others from being ensnared in the Jewish web of corruption and deceit.

But what to do about the Jews themselves? Here we find a frankly shocking assertion: Chrysostom states very explicitly that the Jews are beasts, and such beasts, "though unfit for work, are fit for killing" (I.2.6). For killing! As if to emphasize the point, he immediately reiterates: "And this is what happened to the Jews: while they were making themselves unfit for work, they grew fit for slaughter." He then cites Jesus himself for justification: "As for these enemies of mine…, bring them here and slay them before me" (Luke 19:27). This is an astounding position to take, especially from such a prominent "man of God." And yet, here it is: there seems to be no other real solution than to rid society completely of its Jews—one way or another.

*****

But are these valid complaints? Chrysostom has a long list of worries, and evidently has, or feels he has, more than enough evidence and practical experience to warrant such conclusions. The fact that such complaints have been repeated, before and since, by dozens of prominent thinkers and writers seems to confirm his stance. Chrysostom is far from alone; he likely felt he was rather mainstream in his thinking, and was only expressing the matter bluntly so as to better prod his listeners into action.

It is true that Jews, both religious and secular, have been largely materialist for millennia. Judaism, as expressed in the Old Testament, is not so much a spiritual tract as a "war-cry in the struggle with other nations," to quote Schopenhauer.[5] Even one of their own, Karl Marx, born into a Jewish family, acknowledged the intrinsic materialism of Jewry:

> What is the profane basis of Judaism? *Practical* need, *self-interest*. What is the worldly cult of the Jews? *Huckstering*. What is his worldly god? *Money*.[6]

As surprising as it may be, Judaism, as expressed in the Old Testament, is virtually devoid of talk of an immortal soul, heaven, or any kind of after-life. As Schopenhauer explains, "The real religion of the Jews…is the crudest of all religions because it is the only one that has absolutely no doctrine of immortality, not even a trace thereof".[7] And again:

> We see [from Tacitus and Justinus] how much the Jews were, at all times and by all nations, loathed and despised. This may be partly due to the fact that they were the only people on earth who did not credit man with any existence beyond this life and were, therefore, regarded as beasts… [Jews are] the scum of humanity—but great master of lies.[8]

Such views, coming some 1,400 years after Chrysostom, confirm his worries. He was not a lone crank; he had insight into the Jewish condition that has been verified in countless ways and by countless observers over the centuries.

---

[5] *Parerga and Paralipomena* (1851), volume 1, p. 126. Reproduced in *Eternal Strangers*, p. 80.
[6] "On the Jewish question" (1843).
[7] Op. cit., note 5.
[8] *Parerga*, volume 2, p. 357.

In fact, one obvious comparison is with Martin Luther, who lived 1,000 years later. Famous as the founder of both Protestantism and the Lutheran Church, Luther was at once a deep and skilled theologian, and a fundamentalist rebel. He witnessed corruption in the Catholic Church circa 1500 AD and sought to return Christianity to its roots. In the process, he also observed, like Chrysostom, the highly detrimental effect of Jews on his German parishioners. This led him, in 1543, to publish the book *On the Jews and Their Lies*, which is a scathing indictment of the Hebrews, both from a theological and a secular viewpoint.[9] If anything, Luther is even harsher than Chrysostom: the Jews "must be driven from our country" because they are "stiff-necked, disobedient, prophet-murderers, arrogant, usurers, and filled with every vice"; and they are "desperate, thoroughly evil, poisonous, and devilish." Indeed, if they refuse to be driven out, then "we are at fault in not slaying them"—an astonishing reiteration of Chrysostom's notorious line about Jews being fit for slaughter. It is highly recommended to read Luther's famous book in conjunction with the present volume.

Finally, it is worth pointing out that, today, we have not so many "Judaizing Christians" as we do "Judaizing Gentiles"—non-Jews of all races and creeds who work with, work for, collaborate with, or provide cover for, Jews. Virtually every Gentile we see on television, in films, or hear on radio are compromised; they are all working with or for wealthy and influential Jews, and are thus helping them to become yet wealthier and more powerful. And all Gentiles in upper levels of politics, especially at the federal level, are likewise totally compromised; they are in positions of power only thanks to Jewish money and Jewish support. Any politician who might oppose the Jewish Lobby is sure to be ousted in the next election. And in fact, this could be the functional definition of an "election": any democratic process by which Jews or their sycophants are elevated to positions of power. (We recall the words of poet Ezra Pound: "Democracy is now currently defined as a country run by Jews.")

Hence, the rest of us "bystanders" must heed Chrysostom's call—to call out the Gentile Judaizers, to expose them and their backers, to shine a light on the resulting immorality and criminality, and to lay bare the

---

[9] For a good recent translation, see my updated 2025 edition, *On the Jews and Their Lies*, from Clemens & Blair.

root cause of the corruption. By this process, we aid our fellow man; we can be that very salvation that Chrysostom was so anxious to bestow upon his people. One need not be a Christian to work for the salvation of all.

In sum, we must agree that John Chrysostom has written a remarkable text—at once learned and critical, theological and practical. And like any classic text, it carries a timeless message; in this case—Beware the Jews!

HOMILIES AGAINST
THE JEWS

HOMILY I

(1) My intent today was to complete my discussion on the topic that I addressed to you a few days ago; I wanted to present you with even clearer proof that God's nature is more than our minds can grasp. Last Sunday, I spoke on this at great length and I brought forward as my witnesses Isaiah, David, and Paul. For it was Isaiah who exclaimed: "Yet who of his generation protested?"[1] David knew God was beyond his comprehension and so he gave thanks to him and said: "I praise thee, for thou art fearful and wonderful. Wonderful are thy works!".[2] And again it was David who said: "Such knowledge is too wonderful for me; it is high, I cannot attain it".[3] Paul did not search and pry into God's very essence, but only into his providence; I should say rather that he looked only on the small portion of divine providence which God had made manifest when he called the gentiles. And Paul saw this small part as a vast and incomprehensible sea when he exclaimed: "O the depth of the riches and wisdom and knowledge of God! How unsearchable are his judgments and how inscrutable his ways!"[4]

(2) These three witnesses gave us enough proof, but I was not satisfied with prophets nor did I settle for apostles. I mounted to the heavens and gave you as proof the chorus of angels as they sang: "Glory to God in the highest, and on earth peace among men with whom he is pleased!".[5] Again, you heard the Seraphim as they shuddered and cried out in astonishment: "Holy, holy, holy is the Lord of hosts; the whole earth is full of his glory".[6] And I gave you also the cherubim who exclaimed: "Blessed be his glory in his dwelling".

---

[1] Isa. 53:8 (New International Version; remaining quotations will use Revised Standard Version, unless otherwise stated.)
[2] Ps. 139:14
[3] Ps. 139:6
[4] Rom. 11:33
[5] Luke 2:14
[6] Isa. 6:3

(3) Hence there were three witnesses on Earth and three in Heaven who made it clear that God's glory cannot be approached. For the rest, the proof was beyond dispute; there was great applause, the audience warmed with enthusiasm, you assembly came aflame. I did rejoice at this, yet my joy was not because praise was coming to me but because glory was coming to my Master. For that applause and praise showed the love you have for God in your souls. If a servant loves his master and hears someone speak in praise of that master, his heart comes aflame with a love for him who speaks. This is because the servant loves his master. You acted just that way when I spoke: by the abundance of your applause, you showed clearly your abundant love for the Master.

(4) And thus I wanted again today to engage in that contest. For if the enemies of the truth never have enough of blaspheming our Benefactor, we must be all the more tireless in praising the God of all. But what am I to do? Another very serious illness calls for any cure my words can bring, an illness which has become implanted in the body of the Church. We must first root this ailment out and then take thought for matters outside; we must first cure our own and then be concerned for others who are strangers.

(5) What is this disease? The festivals of the pitiful and miserable Jews are soon to march upon us one after the other and in quick succession: the feast of Trumpets, the feast of Tabernacles, the fasts. There are many in our ranks who say they think as we do. Yet some of these are going to watch the festivals and others will join the Jews in keeping their feasts and observing their fasts. I wish to drive this perverse custom from the Church right now. My homilies against the Anomians can be put off to another time, and the postponement would cause no harm.[7] But now that the Jewish festivals are close by and at the very door, if I should fail to cure those who are sick with the Judaizing disease, I am afraid that, because of their ill-suited association and deep ignorance, some Christians may partake in the Jews' transgressions. And once they have done so, I fear my homilies on these transgressions will be in vain. For if they hear no word from me today, they will then join the Jews in their fasts;

---

[7] The Anomians were a subset of the Arians (no connection to 'Aryans'), who disputed the divinity of Jesus.

once they have committed this sin it will be useless for me to apply the remedy.

(6) And so it is that I hasten to anticipate this danger and prevent it. This is what physicians do. They first check the diseases which are most urgent and acute. But the danger from this sickness is very closely related to the danger from the other; since the Anomians impiety is akin to that of the Jews, my present conflict is akin to my former one. And there is a kinship because the Jews and the Anomians make the same accusation. And what charges do the Jews make? That He called God His own Father and so made Himself equal to God. The Anomians also make this charge—I should not say they make this a charge; they even blot out the phrase "equal to God" and what it connotes, by their resolve to reject it even if they do not physically erase it.

II

(1) But do not be surprised that I called the Jews pitiable. They really are pitiable and miserable. When so many blessings from heaven came into their hands, they thrust them aside and were at great pains to reject them. The morning Sun of Justice arose for them, but they thrust aside its rays and still sit in darkness. We, who were nurtured by darkness, drew the light to ourselves and were freed from the gloom of their error. They were the branches of that holy root, but those branches were broken. We had no share in the root, but we did reap the fruit of godliness. From their childhood they read the prophets, but they crucified him whom the prophets had foretold. We did not hear the divine prophecies but we did worship him of whom they prophesied. And so they are pitiful because they rejected the blessings which were sent to them, while others seized hold of these blessing and drew them to themselves. Although those Jews had been called to the adoption of sons, they fell to kinship with dogs; we who were dogs received the strength, through God's grace, to put aside the irrational nature which was ours and to rise to the honor of sons. How do I prove this? Christ said: "It is not fair to take the children's bread and throw it to the dogs".[8] Christ was speaking to the Canaanite woman when He called the Jews 'children' and the Gentiles 'dogs.'

---

[8] Matt. 15:26

(2) But see how thereafter the order was changed about: they became dogs, and we became the children. Paul said of the Jews: "Look out for the dogs, look out for the evil-workers, look out for those who mutilate the flesh. For we are the true circumcision".[9] Do you see how those who at first were children became dogs? Do you wish to find out how we, who at first were dogs, became children? "But to all who received him, who believed in his name, he gave power to become children of God".[10]

(3) Nothing is more miserable than those people who never failed to attack their own salvation. When there was need to observe the Law, they trampled it under foot. Now that the Law has ceased to bind, they obstinately strive to observe it. What could be more pitiable that those who provoke God not only by transgressing the Law but also by keeping it? On this account, Stephen said: "You stiff-necked people, uncircumcised in heart and ears, you always resist the Holy Spirit",[11] not only by transgressing the Law but also by wishing to observe it at the wrong time.

(4) Stephen was right in calling them stiff-necked. For they failed to take up the yoke of Christ, although it was sweet and had nothing about it which was either burdensome or oppressive. For he said: "Take my yoke upon you, and learn from me; for I am gentle and lowly in heart",[12] and "For my yoke is easy, and my burden is light".[13] Nonetheless they failed to take up the yoke because of the stiffness of their necks. Not only did they fail to take it up but they broke it and destroyed it. For Jeremiah said: "For long ago you broke your yoke and burst your bonds ".[14] It was not Paul who said this but the voice of the prophet speaking loud and clear. When he spoke of the yoke and the bonds, he meant the symbols of rule, because the Jews rejected the rule of Christ when they said: "We have no king but Caesar".[15] You Jews broke the yoke, you burst the bonds, you cast yourselves out of the kingdom of heaven, and you made yourselves subject to the rule of men. Please consider with me how accurately the prophet hinted that their hearts were uncontrolled. He did not

---

[9] Phil. 3:2
[10] John 1:12
[11] Acts 7:51
[12] Matt. 11:29
[13] Matt. 11:30
[14] Jer. 2:20
[15] John 19:15

say: "You set aside the yoke," but "You broke the yoke" and this is the crime of untamed beasts, who are uncontrolled and reject rule.

(5) But what is the source of this hardness? It come from gluttony and drunkenness. Who say so? Moses himself. "Israel ate and was filled and the darling grew fat and frisky".[16] When brute animals feed from a full manger, they grow plump and become more obstinate and hard to hold in check; they endure neither the yoke, the reins, nor the hand of the charioteer. Just so the Jewish people were driven by their drunkenness and plumpness to the ultimate evil; they kicked about, they failed to accept the yoke of Christ, nor did they pull the plow of his teaching. Another prophet hinted at this when he said: "Like a stubborn heifer, Israel is stubborn".[17] And still another called the Jews "an untamed calf".

(6) Although such beasts are unfit for work, they are fit for killing. And this is what happened to the Jews: while they were making themselves unfit for work, they grew fit for slaughter.[18] This is why Christ said: "But as for these enemies of mine, who did not want me to reign over them, bring them here and slay them before me".[19] You Jews should have fasted then, when drunkenness was doing those terrible things to you, when your gluttony was giving birth to your ungodliness—not now. Now your fasting is untimely and an abomination. Who said so? Isaiah himself when he called out in a loud voice: "Is not this the fast that I choose".[20] Why? "Behold, you fast only to quarrel and to fight and to hit with wicked fist".[21] But if your fasting was an abomination when you were striking your fellow slaves, does it become acceptable now that you have slain your Master? How could that be right?

(7) The man who fasts should be properly restrained, contrite, humbled—not drunk with anger. But do you strike your fellow slaves? In Isaiah's day they quarreled and squabbled when they fasted; now when they fast, they go in for excesses and the ultimate licentiousness, dancing with bare feet in the marketplace. The pretext is that they are fasting, but

---

[16] Deut 32:15

[17] Hosea 4:16

[18] A remarkably blunt statement by Chrysostom, and perhaps the first Christian-era call to kill Jews.

[19] Luke 19:27

[20] Isa. 58:6

[21] Isa. 58:4

they act like men who are drunk. Hear how the prophet bid them to fast. "Sanctify a fast",[22] he said. He did not say: "Make a parade of your fasting", but "call a solemn assembly. Gather the elders".[23] But these Jews are gathering choruses of effeminates and a great rubbish heap of harlots; they drag into the synagogue the whole theater, actors and all. For there is no difference between the theater and the synagogue. I know that some suspect me of rashness because I said there is no difference between the theater and the synagogue; but I suspect them of rashness if they do not think that this is so. If my declaration that the two are the same rests on my own authority, then charge me with rashness. But if the words I speak are the words of the prophet, then accept his decision.

III

(1) Many, I know, respect the Jews and think that their present way of life is a venerable one. This is why I hasten to uproot and tear out this deadly opinion. I said that the synagogue is no better than a theater and I bring forward a prophet as my witness. Surely the Jews are not more deserving of belief than their prophets. "Yet you have a harlot's brow, you refuse to be ashamed".[24] Where a harlot has set herself up, that place is a brothel. But the synagogue is not only a brothel and a theater; it also is a den of robbers and a lodging for wild beasts. Jeremiah said: "My land has become a lair for hyenas".[25] He does not simply say "of a wild beast," but "of a filthy wild beast," and again: "I have forsaken my house, I have abandoned my heritage".[26] But when God forsakes a people, what hope of salvation is left? When God forsakes a place, that place becomes the dwelling of demons.

(2) But at any rate, the Jews say that they, too, adore God. God forbid that I say that. No Jew adores God! Who says so? The Son of God says so. For he said: "You know neither me nor my Father; if you knew me, you would know my Father also".[27] Could I produce a witness more trustworthy than the Son of God?

---

[22] Joel 1:14
[23] Joel 1:14
[24] Jer. 3:3
[25] Jer. 12:9 (NCB)
[26] Jer. 12:7
[27] John 8:19

(3) If, then, the Jews fail to know the Father, if they crucified the Son, if they thrust off the help of the Spirit, who should not make bold to declare plainly that the synagogue is a dwelling of demons? God is not worshipped there. Heaven forbid! From now on it remains a place of idolatry. But still some people pay it honor as a holy place.

(4) Let me tell you this, not from guesswork but from my own experience. Three days ago—believe me, I am not lying—I saw a free woman of good bearing, modest, and a believer. A brutal, unfeeling man, reputed to be a Christian (for I would not call a person who would dare to do such a thing a sincere Christian) was forcing her to enter the shrine of the Hebrews and to swear there an oath about some matters under dispute with him. She came up to me and asked for help; she begged me to prevent this lawless violence—for it was forbidden to her, who had shared in the divine mysteries, to enter that place. I was fired with indignation, I became angry, I rose up, I refused to let her be dragged into that transgression, I snatched her from the hands of her abductor. I asked him if he were a Christian, and he said he was. Then I set upon him vigorously, charging him with lack of feeling and the worst stupidity; I told him he was no better off than a mule if he, who professed to worship Christ, would drag someone off to the dens of the Jews who had crucified him. I talked to him a long time, drawing my lesson from the Holy Gospels; I told him first that it was altogether forbidden to swear and that it was wrong to impose the necessity of swearing on anyone. I then told him that he must not subject a baptized believer to this necessity. In fact, he must not force even an unbaptized person to swear an oath.

(5) After I talked with him at great length and had driven the folly of his error from his soul, I asked him why he rejected the Church and dragged the woman to the place where the Hebrews assembled. He answered that many people had told him that oaths sworn there were more to be feared. His words made me groan, then I grew angry, and finally I began to smile. When I saw the devil's wickedness, I groaned because he had the power to seduce men; I grew angry when I considered how careless were those who were deceived; when I saw the extent and depth of the folly of those who were deceived, I smiled.

(6) I told you this story because you are savage and ruthless in your attitude toward those who do such things and undergo these experiences. If you see one of your brothers falling into such transgressions, you con-

sider that it is someone else's misfortune, not your own; you think you have defended yourselves against your accusers when you say: "What concern of mine is it? What do I have in common with that man"? When you say that, your words manifest the utmost hatred for mankind and a cruelty which benefits the devil. What are you saying? You are a man and share the same nature. Why speak of a common nature when you have but a single head, Christ? Do you dare to say you have nothing in common with your own members? In what sense do you admit that Christ is the head of the Church? For certainly it is the function of the head to join all the limbs together, to order them carefully to each other, and to bind them into one nature. But if you have nothing in common with your members, then you have nothing in common with your brother, nor do you have Christ as your head.

(7) The Jews frighten you as if you were little children, and you do not see it. Many wicked slaves show frightening and ridiculous masks to youngsters—the masks are not frightening by their nature, but they seem so to the children's simple minds—and in this way they stir up many a laugh. This is the way the Jews frighten the simpler-minded Christians with the bugbears and hobgoblins of their shrines. Yet how could their ridiculous and disgraceful synagogues frighten you? Are they not the shrines of men who have been rejected, dishonored, and condemned?

IV

(1) Our churches are not like that; they are truly frightening and filled with fear. God's presence makes a place frightening because he has power over life and death. In our churches we hear countless homilies on eternal punishments, on rivers of fire, on the venomous worm, on bonds that cannot be burst, or exterior darkness. But the Jews neither know nor dream of these things. They live for their bellies, they gape for the things of this world, their condition is not better than that of pigs or goats because of their wanton ways and excessive gluttony. They know but one thing: to fill their bellies and be drunk, to get all cut and bruised, to be hurt and wounded while fighting for their favorite charioteers.

(2) Tell me, then, are their shrines awful and frightening? Who would say so? What reasons do we have for thinking that they are frightening unless someone should tell us that dishonored slaves, who have no right to speak and who have been driven from their Master's home,

should frighten us, who have been given honor and the freedom to speak? Certainly this is not the case. Inns are not more august than royal palaces. Indeed, the synagogue is less deserving of honor than any inn. It is not merely a lodging place for robbers and cheats but also for demons. This is true not only of the synagogues but also of the souls of the Jews, as I shall try to prove at the end of my homily.

(3) I urge you to keep my words in your minds in a special way. For I am not now speaking for show or applause but to cure your souls. And what else is left for me to say when some of you are still sick, even though there are so many physicians to effect a cure?

(4) There were twelve apostles and they drew the whole world to themselves.[28] The greater portion of the city is Christian, yet some are still sick with the Judaizing disease. And what could we, who are healthy, say in our own defense? Surely those who are sick deserve to be accused. But we are not free from blame, because we have neglected them in their hour of illness; if we had shown great concern for them and they had the benefit of this care, they could not possibly still be sick.

(5) Let me get the start on you by saying this now, so that each of you may win over his brother. Even if you must impose restraint, even if you must use force, even if you must treat him ill and obstinately, do everything to save him from the devil's snare and to free him from fellowship with those who slew Christ.

(6) Tell me this. Suppose you were to see a man who had been justly condemned being led to execution through the marketplace. Suppose it were in your power to save him from the hands of the public executioner. Would you not do all you could to keep him from being dragged off? But now you see your own brother being dragged off unjustly to the depth of destruction. And it is not the executioner who drags him of, but the devil. Would you be so bold as not to do your part toward rescuing him from his transgression? If you don't help him, what excuse would you find? But your brother is stronger and more powerful than you. Show him to me. If he will stand fast in his obstinate resolve, I shall choose to risk my life rather than let him enter the doors of the synagogue.

---

[28] Although, it is unclear who exactly those twelve were. We get different lists of names from Mark (3:16), Matthew (10:2), Luke (6:14), and John.

(7) I shall say to him: What fellowship do you have with the free Jerusalem, with the Jerusalem above? You chose the one below; be a slave with that earthly Jerusalem which, according to the word of the Apostle, is a slave together with her children. Do you fast with the Jews? Then take off your shoes with the Jews, and walk barefoot in the market-place, and share with them in their indecency and laughter. But you would not choose to do this because you are ashamed and apt to blush. Are you ashamed to share with them in outward appearance but una-shamed to share in their impiety? What excuse will you have, you who are only half a Christian?

(8) Believe me, I shall risk my life before I would neglect anyone who is sick with this disease—if I see him. If I fail to see him, surely God will grant me pardon. And let each one of you consider this matter; let him not think it is something of secondary importance. Do you take no notice of what the deacon continuously calls out in the mysteries? "Rec-ognize one another," he says. Do you not see how he entrusts to you the careful examination of your brothers? Do this in the case of Judaizers, too. When you observe someone Judaizing, take hold of him, show him what he is doing, so that you may not yourself be an accessory to the risk he runs.

(9) If any Roman soldier serving overseas is caught favoring the barbarians and the Persians, not only is he in danger but so also is every-one who was aware of how this felt and failed to make this fact known to the general. Since you are the army of Christ, be overly careful in search-ing to see if anyone favoring an alien faith has mingled among you, and make his presence known—not so that we may put him to death, as those generals did, nor that we may punish him or take our vengeance upon him, but that we may free him from his error and ungodliness and make him entirely our own.

(10) If you are unwilling to do this, if you know of such a person but conceal him, be sure that both you and he will be subject to the same penalty. For Paul subjects to chastisement and punishment not only those who commit acts of wickedness but also those who approve what they have done. The prophet, too, brings to the same judgment not only thieves but also those who run with the thieves. And this is quite reason-able. For if a man is aware of a criminal's actions but covers them up and

conceals them, he is providing a stronger basis for the criminal to be careless of the law and making him less afraid in his career of crime.

V

(1) But I must get back again to those who are sick. Consider, then, with whom they are sharing their fasts. It is with those who shouted: "Crucify, crucify him!",[29] with those who said: "His blood be on us and on our children".[30] If some men had been caught in rebellion against their ruler and were condemned, would you have dared to go up to them and to speak with them? I think not. Is it not foolish, then, to show such readiness to flee from those who have sinned against a man, but to enter into fellowship with those who have committed outrages against God himself? Is it not strange that those who worship the Crucified keep common festival with those who crucified him? Is it not a sign of folly and the worst madness?

(2) Since there are some who think of the synagogue as a holy place, I must say a few words to them. Why do you reverence that place? Must you not despise it, hold it in abomination, run away from it? They answer that the Law and the books of the prophets are kept there. What is this? Will any place where these books are be a holy place? By no means! This is the reason above all others why I hate the synagogue and abhor it. They have the prophets but not believe them; they read the sacred writings but reject their witness—and this is a mark of men guilty of the greatest outrage.

(3) Tell me this. If you were to see a venerable man, illustrious and renowned, dragged off into a tavern or den of robbers; if you were to see him outraged, beaten, and subjected there to the worst violence, would you have held that tavern or den in high esteem because that great and esteemed man had been inside it while undergoing that violent treatment? I think not. Rather, for this very reason you would have hated and abhorred the place.

(4) Let that be your judgment about the synagogue, too. For they brought the books of Moses and the prophets along with them into the synagogue, not to honor them but to outrage them with dishonor. When

---

[29] Luke 23:21, Mark 15:13, John 19:6.
[30] Matt. 27:25

they say that Moses and the prophets knew not Christ and said nothing about his coming, what greater outrage could they do to those holy men than to accuse them of failing to recognize their Master, than to say that those saintly prophets are partners of their impiety? And so it is that we must hate both them and their synagogue all the more because of their offensive treatment of those holy men.

(5) Why do I speak about the books and the synagogues? In time of persecution, the public executioners lay hold of the bodies of the martyrs, they scourge them, and tear them to pieces. Does it make the executioners' hands holy because they lay hold of the body of holy men? Heaven forbid! The hands which grasped and held the bodies of the holy ones still stay unholy. Why? Because those executioners did a wicked thing when they laid their hands upon the holy. And will those who handle and outrage the writings of the holy ones be any more venerable for this than those who executed the martyrs? Would that not be the ultimate foolishness? If the maltreated bodies of the martyrs do not sanctify those who maltreated them but even add to their blood-guilt, much less could the Scriptures, if read without belief, ever help those who read without believing. The very act of deliberately choosing to maltreat the Scriptures convicts them of greater godlessness.

(6) If they did not have the prophets, they would not deserve such punishment; if they had not read the sacred books, they would not be so unclean and so unholy. But, as it is, they have been stripped of all excuse. They do have the heralds of the truth but, with hostile heart, they set themselves against the prophets and the truth they speak. So it is for this reason that they would be all the more profane and blood-guilty; they have the prophets, but they treat them with hostile hearts.

(7) So it is that I exhort you to flee and shun their gatherings. The harm they bring to our weaker brothers is not slight; they offer no slight excuse to sustain to the folly of the Jews. For when they see that you, who worship the Christ whom they crucified, are reverently following their rituals, how can they fail to think that the rites they have performed are the best and that our ceremonies are worthless? For after you worship and adore at our mysteries, you run to the very men who destroy our rites. Paul said: "For if anyone sees you, a man of knowledge, at table in an idol's temple, might he not be encouraged, if his conscience is weak,

to eat food offered to idols"?[31] And let me say: If a man sees you that have knowledge come into the synagogue and participate in the festival of the Trumpets, shall not his conscience, being weak, be emboldened to admire what the Jews do? He who falls not only pays the penalty for his own fall, but he is also punished because he trips others as well. But the man who has stood firm is rewarded, not only because of his own virtue but people admire him for leading others to desire the same things.

(8) Therefore, flee the gatherings and holy places of the Jews. Let no man venerate the synagogue because of the holy books; let him hate and avoid it because the Jews outrage and maltreat the holy ones, because they refuse to believe their words, because they accuse them of the ultimate impiety.

VI

(1) That you may know that the sacred books do not make a place holy but that the purpose of those who frequent a place does make it profane, I shall tell an old story. Ptolemy Philadelphus had collected books from all over the world.[32] When he learned that the Jews had writings which treated of God and the ideal state, he sent for men from Judea and had them translate those books, which he then had deposited in the temple of Serapis, for he was a pagan. Up to the present day, the translated books remain there in the temple. But will the temple of Serapis be holy because of the holy books? Heaven forbid! Although the books have their own holiness, they do not give a share of it to the place because those who frequent the place are defiled.

(2) You must apply the same argument to the synagogue. Even if there is no idol there, still demons do inhabit the place. And I say this not only about the synagogue here in town [Antioch] but about the one in Daphne as well; for at Daphne you have a more wicked place of perdition which they call Matrona's.[33] I have heard that many of the faithful go up there and sleep beside the place.

(3) But heaven forbid that I call these people faithful. For to me, the shrine of Matrona and the temple of Apollo are equally profane. If anyone

---

[31] 1 Cor. 8:10

[32] A reference to Ptolemy II (309-246 BC), pharaoh of Egypt.

[33] Daphne was a wealthy suburb of Antioch. The "shrine" (cave) of Matrona was a widely-known Jewish healing site.

charges me with boldness, I will in turn charge him with the utmost madness. For, tell me, is not the dwelling place of demons a place of impiety even if no god's statue stands there? Here the slayers of Christ gather together, here the cross is driven out, here God is blasphemed, here the Father is ignored, here the Son is outraged, here the grace of the Spirit is rejected. Does not greater harm come from this place since the Jews themselves are demons? In the pagan temple the impiety is naked and obvious; it would not be ease to deceive a man of sound and prudent mind or entice him to go there. But in the synagogue, there are men who say they worship God and abhor idols, men who say they have prophets and pay them honor. But by their words they make ready an abundance of bait to catch in their nets the simpler souls who are so foolish as to be caught off guard.

(4) Thus, the godlessness of the Jews and the pagans is on a par. But the Jews practice a deceit which is more dangerous. In their synagogue stands an invisible altar of deceit on which they sacrifice not sheep and calves but the souls of men.

(5) Finally, if the ceremonies of the Jews move you to admiration, what do you have in common with us? If the Jewish ceremonies are venerable and great, ours are lies. But if ours are true, as they *are* true, theirs are filled with deceit. I am not speaking of the Scriptures. Heaven forbid! It was the Scriptures which took me by the hand and led me to Christ. But I am talking about the ungodliness and present madness of the Jews.

(6) Certainly it is the time for me to show that demons dwell in the synagogue, not only in the place itself but also in the souls of the Jews. As Christ said:

> When the unclean spirit has gone out of a man, he passes through waterless places seeking rest, but he finds none. Then he says, "I will return to my house from which I came." And when he comes he finds it empty, swept, and put in order. Then he goes and brings with him seven other spirits more evil than himself, and they enter and dwell there; and the last state of that man becomes worse than the first. So shall it be also with this evil generation.[34]

---

[34] Matt. 12:43-45

(7) Do you see that demons dwell in their souls and that these demons are more dangerous than the ones of old? And this is very reasonable. In the old days, the Jews acted impiously toward the prophets; now they outrage the Master of the prophets. Tell me this. Do you not shudder to come into the same place with men possessed, who have so many unclean spirits, who have been reared amid slaughter and bloodshed? Must you share a greeting with them and exchange a bare word? Must you not turn away from them since they are the common disgrace and infection of the whole world? Have they not come to every form of wickedness? Have not all the prophets spent themselves making many and long speeches of accusation against them? What tragedy, what manner of lawlessness have they not eclipsed by their blood-guiltiness? They sacrificed their own sons and daughters to demons.[35] They refused to recognize nature, they forgot the pangs of birth, they trod underfoot the rearing of their children, they overturned from their foundations the laws of kingship, they became more savage than any wild beast.

(8) Wild beasts oftentimes lay down their lives and scorn their own safety to protect their young. No necessity forced the Jews when they slew their own children with their own hands to pay honor to the avenging demons, the foes of our life.[36] What deed of theirs should strike us with greater astonishment? Their ungodliness or their cruelty or their inhumanity? That they sacrificed their children or that they sacrificed them to demons? Because of their licentiousness, did they not show a lust beyond that of irrational animals? Hear what the prophet says of their excesses. "They were well-fed lusty stallions, each neighing for his neighbor's wife".[37] He did not say: "Everyone lusted after his neighbor's wife," but he expressed the madness which came from their licentiousness with the greatest clarity by speaking of it as the neighing of brute beasts.

VII

(1) What else do you want to hear? Shall I tell you of their plundering, their covetousness, their abandonment of the poor, their thefts, their cheating in trade? the whole day long will not be enough to give you an

---

[35] Ps. 106:37.
[36] See also 2 Kings 6:24-30, where Jewish women kill and eat their own children, amidst a famine.
[37] Jer. 5:8

account of these things. But do their festivals have something solemn and great about them? They have shown that these, too, are impure. Listen to the prophets; rather, listen to God and with how strong a statement he turns his back on them: "I hate, I despise your feasts, and I take no delight in your solemn assemblies".[38]

(2) Does God hate their festivals and do you share in them? He did not say this or that festival, but all of them together. Do you wish to see that God hates the worship paid with kettledrums, with lyres, with harps, and other instruments? God said: "Take away from me the noise of your songs; to the melody of your harps, I will not listen".[39] If God said: "Take them away from me", do you run to listen to the trumpets? Are these sacrifices and offerings not an abomination? "Bring no more vain offerings; incense is an abomination to me".[40] The incense is an abomination. Is not the place also an abomination? Before they committed the crime of crimes, before they killed their Master, before the cross, before the slaying of Christ, it was an abomination. Is it not now all the more an abomination? And yet what is more fragrant than incense? But God looks not to the nature of the gifts but to the intention of those who bring them; it is this intention that he judges their offerings.

(3) He paid heed to Abel and then to his gifts. He looked at Cain and then turned away from his offering. For Scripture says: "But for Cain and his offering he had no regard".[41] Noah offered to God sacrifices of sheep and calves and birds. The Scripture say: "And when the Lord smelled the pleasing odor",[42] that is, he accepted the offerings. For God has no nostrils but is a bodiless spirit. Yet what is carried up from the altar is the odor and smoke from burning bodies, and nothing is more malodorous than such a savor.[43] But that you may learn that God attends to the intention of the one offering the sacrifice and then accepts or rejects it, Scripture calls the odor and the smoke a sweet savor; but it calls

---

[38] Amos 5:21

[39] Amos 5:23

[40] Isa. 1:13

[41] Gen. 4:5

[42] Gen. 8:21

[43] The Jews were infamous for slaughtering and burning animals in their temples —by the dozens, every day.

the incense an abomination because the intention of those offering it reeked with a great stench.

(4) Do you wish to learn that, together with the sacrifices and the musical instruments and the festivals and the incense, God also rejects the temple because of those who enter it? He showed this mostly by his deeds, when he gave it over to barbarian hands, and later when he utterly destroyed it.[44] But even before its destruction, through his prophet he shouted aloud and said: "Do not trust in these deceptive words: 'This is the temple of the Lord, the temple of the Lord, the temple of the Lord'".[45] What the prophet says is that the temple does not make holy those who gather there, but those who gather there make the temple holy. If the temple did not help at a time when the Cherubim and the Ark were there, much less will it help now that all those things are gone, now that God's rejection is complete, now that there is greater ground for enmity. How great an act of madness and derangement would it be to take as your partners in the festivals those who have been dishonored, those whom God has forsaken, those who angered the Master?

(5) Tell me this. If a man were to have slain your son, would you endure to look upon him, or accept his greeting? Would you not shun him as a wicked demon, as the devil himself? They slew the Son of your Lord; do you have the boldness to enter with them under the same roof? After he was slain, he heaped such honor upon you that he made you his brother and co-heir. But you dishonor him so much that you pay honor to those who slew him on the cross, that you observe with them the fellowship of the festivals, that you go to their profane places, enter their unclean doors, and share in the tables of demons. For I am persuaded to call the fasting of the Jews 'a table of demons' because they slew God.

If the Jews are acting against God, must they not be serving the demons? Are you looking for demons to cure you? When Christ allowed the demons to enter into the swine, straightway they plunged into the sea.[46] Will these demons spare the bodies of men? I wish they would not kill men's bodies, that they would not plot against them. But they will. The demons cast men from Paradise and deprived them the honor from above. Will they cure their bodies? That is ridiculous, mere stories. The

---

[44] Actually, the Romans destroyed the Jewish temple at Jerusalem in 70 AD.
[45] Jer. 7:4
[46] See, for example, Matthew 8:28-34.

demons know how to plot and do harm, not to cure. They do not spare souls. Tell me, then, will they spare bodies? They try to drive men from the Kingdom. Will they choose to free them from disease?

(6) Did you not hear what the prophet said? Rather, did you hear what God said through the prophet? He said that the demons can do neither good nor evil. Even if they could cure and wanted to do so—which is impossible—you must not take an indestructible and unending punishment in exchange for a slight benefit which can soon be destroyed. Will you cure your body and destroy your soul? You are making a poor exchange. Are you angering God who made your body, and are you calling to your aid the demon who plots against you?

(7) If any demon-fearing pagan has medical knowledge, will he also find it easy to win you over to worship the pagan gods? Those pagans, too, have their skill. They, too, have often cured many diseases and brought the sick back to health. Are we going to share in their godlessness on this account? Heaven forbid! Hear what Moses said to the Jews.

> If a prophet arises among you, or a dreamer of dreams, and gives you a sign or a wonder, and the sign or wonder which he tells you comes to pass, and if he says, "Let us go after other gods," which you have not known, "and let us serve them," you shall not listen to the words of that prophet or to that dreamer of dreams.[47]

(8) What Moses means is this. If some prophet rises up, he says, and performs a sign, by either raising a dead man or cleansing a leper, or curing a maimed man, and after working the wonder calls you to impiety, do not heed him just because his sign comes to pass. Why? "The Lord your God is trying you to see whether you love him with all your heart and all your soul".[48] From this it is clear that demons do not cure. If ever God should permit demons to cure, as he might permit a man to do, his permission is given to test you—not because God does not know what you are, but that he may teach you to reject even the demons who do cure.

---

[47] Deut. 13:1-3
[48] Deut. 13:3

(9) And why do I speak of bodily cures? If any man threatens you with Gehenna unless you deny Christ, do not heed his words.[49] If someone should promise you a kingdom to revolt from the only-begotten Son of God, turn away from him and hate him. Be a disciple of Paul and emulate those words which his blessed and noble soul exclaimed when he said: "For I am sure that neither death, nor life, nor angels, nor principalities, nor things present, nor things to come, nor powers, nor height, nor depth, nor anything else in all creation, will be able to separate us from the love of God in Christ Jesus our Lord".[50]

(10) No angels, nor powers, nor things present, nor things to come, nor any other creature separated Paul from the love of Christ. Do you revolt to cure your body? And what excuse could we find? Certainly we must fear Christ more than Gehenna and desire him more than a kingdom. Even if we be sick, it is better to remain in ill health than to fall into impiety for the sake of a cure; for even if a demon cures you, he has hurt more than he has helped. He has helped the body, which a short time later will altogether die and rot away. But he has hurt the soul, which will never die. Kidnappers often entice little boys by offering them sweets, and cakes, and marbles, and other such things; then they deprive them of their freedom and their very life. So, too, the demons promise cure of a limb and then dash the whole salvation of the soul into the sea.

(11) Beloved, let us not put up with that; in every way let us seek to keep ourselves free from godlessness. Could Job not have heeded his wife, blasphemed against God, and been free from the disaster which beset him? "Curse God, and die," she said.[51] But he chose to suffer the pain and to waste away; he chose to endure that unbearable blow rather to blaspheme and be free from the evils which beset him. You must emulate him. If the demon shall promise you ten thousand cures from the ills which beset you, do not heed him, do not put up with him—just as Job refused to heed his wife. Chose to endure your illness rather than destroy your faith and the salvation of your soul. God does not forsake you. It is because he wishes to increase your glory that oftentimes he permits you to fall sick. Keep up your courage so that you may also hear him say:

---

[49] 'Gehenna' (Sheol, Hades) are taken as synonyms of 'hell.'
[50] Rom. 8:38-39
[51] Job 2:9

"Do you think I have dealt with you otherwise than that you may be shown to be just"?

VIII

(1) I could have said more than this, but to keep you from forgetting what I have said, I shall bring my homily to an end here with the words of Moses: "I call heaven and earth to witness against you".[52] If any of you, whether you are here present or not, shall go to the spectacle of the Trumpets, or rush off to the synagogue, or go up to the shrine of Matrona, or take part in fasting, or share in the Sabbath, or observe any other Jewish ritual great or small, I call heaven and earth as my witnesses that I am guiltless of the blood of all of you.

(2) These words will stand by your side and mine on the day of our Lord Jesus Christ. If you heed them, they will bring you great confidence; if you heed them not or conceal anyone who dares to do those things, my words shall stand against you as bitter accusations. "For I did not shrink from declaring to you the whole counsel of God".[53]

(3) I have deposited the money with the bankers. It remains for you to increase the deposit and to use the profit from my words for the salvation of your brothers. Do you find it an oppressive burden to denounce those who commit these sins? It is an oppressive burden to remain silent. For this silence makes you an enemy to God and brings destruction both to you who conceal such sinners and to those whose sins go unrevealed. How much better it is to become hateful to our fellow servants for saving them to provoke God's anger against yourselves. Even if your fellow servant be vexed with you now, he will not be able to harm you but will be grateful later on for his cure. But if you seek to win your fellow servant's favor, if you remain silent and hurt him by concealing his sin, God will exact from you the ultimate penalty. Your silence will make God your foe and will hurt your brother; if you denounce him and reveal his sin, you will make God propitious and benefit your brother and you will gain as a friend one who was crazed but who learned from experience that you served him well.

---

[52] Deut. 30:19
[53] Acts 20:27

(4) Do not think, then, that you are doing your brothers a favor if you should see them pursuing some absurdity and should fail to accuse them with all zeal. If you lose a cloak, do you not consider as your foe not only the one who stole it but also the man who knew of the theft and refused to denounce the thief? Our common Mother (the Church) has lost not a cloak but a brother. The devil stole him and now holds him in Judaism. You know who stole him; you know him who was stolen. Do you see me lighting, as it were, the lamp of my instruction and searching everywhere in my grief? And do you stand silent, refusing to denounce him? What excuse will you have? Will the Church not reckon you among her worst enemies? Will she not consider you a foe and destroyer?

(5) Heaven forbid that anyone who hears my words of advice should commit such a sin as to betray the brother for whom Christ died. Christ poured out his blood on his account. Are you too reluctant to utter a word on this account? I urge you not to be so reluctant. Right after you leave here, stir yourselves to the chase and let each of you bring me one of those suffering from this disease.

(6) But heaven forbid that so many be sick with it. Let two or three, or ten or twenty of you bring me one man. One the day you do and when I see in your nets the game you have caught, I will set before you a more plentiful table. If I see that the advice I gave today has been put to work, I shall be more zealous in undertaking the cure of those men, and this will be a greater boon both for you and them.

(7) Do not regard my words lightly. Be scrupulous in hunting out those who suffer from this sickness. Let the women search for the women, the men for the men, the slaves for the slaves, the freemen for the freemen, and the children for the children. Come all of you to our next meeting with such success that you win praise from me—and, before any praise of mine, that you obtain, from God a great and indescribable reward which in abundant measure surpasses the labors of those who succeed. May all of us obtain this by the grace and loving-kindness of our Lord Jesus Christ, through whom and with whom be glory to the Father together with the Holy Spirit now and forever, world without end. Amen.

HOMILY II

(1) The evil and unclean fast of the Jews is now upon us. Though it is a fast, do not wonder that I have called it unclean. What is done contrary to God's purpose, be it sacrifice or fast, is the most abominable of all things. Their wicked fast will begin after five days. Ten days ago, or more than ten, I anticipated this and gave an exhortation with the hope it would make your brothers safe.[1] Let no one find fault and say my discourse was untimely because I gave it so many days beforehand. When a fever threatens, or any other disease, physicians anticipate this and with many remedies make safe and secure the body of the man who will be seized by the fever; they hurry to snatch his body from the dangers which threaten it before the patient experiences their onset.

(2) Since I, too, see that a very serious disease is going to come upon you, long beforehand I gave you solemn warning so that you might apply corrective measures before the evil attacked. This was my reason for not waiting until just before the days of fasting to exhort you. I did not want the lack of time to stop you from hunting out your brothers; I hoped that with the span of many days, you might be able to track down with all fearlessness those who are suffering from this disease and restore them to health.

(3) Men who are going to celebrate a wedding or prepare a sumptuous feast do this same thing. They do not wait for the day itself. Long beforehand, they speak with the fishermen and bird-hunters so that the brevity of time may present no obstacle to preparing for the banquet. Since I, too, am going to set a banquet before you against the obstinacy of the Jews, I have gotten a head start in talking to you, the fishermen, that you may sweep up your weaker brothers in your nets and bring them to hear what I have to say.

(4) Those of you who did fish and have your catch securely in your nets, remain steadfast and bind them tight with your words of exhortation. Those of you who have not yet taken this goodly catch have time enough in these five days to trap and overcome your prey. So let us

---

[1] That is, Homily I.

spread out the nets of instruction; like a pack of hunting dogs, let us circle about and surround our quarry; let us drive them together from every side and bring them into subjection to the laws of the Church. If you think it is a good idea, let us send to pursue them the best of huntsmen, the blessed Paul, who once shouted aloud and said: "Now I, Paul, say to you that if you receive circumcision, Christ will be of no advantage to you".[2]

(5) When wild beasts and savage animals are hiding under a thicket and hear the shout of the hunter, they leap up in fear. The loud clamor drives them from their hiding and, even against their will, the hunter's cry forces them out, and many a time they fall right into the nets. So, too, your brothers are hiding in what I might call the thicket of Judaism. If they hear the shout of Paul, I am sure that they will easily fall into the nets of salvation and will put aside all the error of the Jews. For it is not Paul who spoke, but Christ, who moved Paul's soul. So when you hear him shout and say: "Now I, Paul, say to you" consider that only the shout is Paul's; the thought and the teaching are Christ's, who is speaking to Paul from within his heart.

(6) But someone might say: "Is there so much harm in circumcision that it makes Christ's whole plan of redemption useless?" Yes, the harm of circumcision is as great as that, not because of its own but because of your obstinacy. There was a time when the law was useful and necessary, but now it has ceased and is fruitless. If you take it on yourself to be circumcised now, when the time is no longer right, it makes the gift of God useless. It is because you are not willing to come to him that Christ will be of no advantage to you.

Suppose someone should be caught in the act of adultery and the foulest crimes and then be thrown into prison. Suppose, next, that judgment was going to be passed against him and that he would be condemned. Suppose that, just at that moment, a letter should come from the Emperor setting free from any accounting or examination all those detained in prison. If the prisoner should refuse to take advantage of the pardon, remain obstinate and choose to be brought to trial, to give an account, and to undergo punishment, he will not be able thereafter to avail himself of the Emperor's favor. For when he made himself accountable

---

[2] Gal. 5:2

to the court, examination, and sentence, he chose of his own accord to deprive himself of the imperial gift.

(7) This is what happened in the case of the Jews. Look how it is. All human nature was taken in the foulest evils. "All have sinned",[3] says Paul. They were locked, as it were, in a prison by the curse of their transgression of the Law. The sentence of the judge was going to be passed against them. A letter from the King came down from heaven. Rather, the King himself came. Without examination, without exacting an account, he set all men free from the claims of their sin.

II

(1) All, then, who run to Christ are saved by his grace and profit from his gift. But those who wish to find justification from the Law will also fall from grace. They will not be able to enjoy the King's loving-kindness because they are striving to gain salvation by their own efforts; they will draw down on themselves the curse of the Law because, from the works of the Law, no flesh will find justification. So it is that Paul says: "If you receive circumcision, Christ will be of no advantage to you".[4] For the man who strives to gain salvation from the works of the Laws has nothing in common with grace. This is what Paul hinted at when he said: "But if it is by grace, it is no longer on the basis of works; otherwise grace would no longer be grace".[5] And again: "For if justification were through the law, then Christ died to no purpose".[6] And again: "You who would be justified by the law; you have fallen away from grace".[7] You have died to the Law, you have become a corpse; hereafter you are no longer under its yoke, you are no longer subject to its necessity. Why, then, do you strive to make trouble for yourself when it is all to no purpose and in vain?

(2) When Paul said: "Now I, Paul, say to you" why did he add his name? Why did he not simply say: "Behold, I tell you"? He wanted to remind them of the zeal which he had shown regarding Judaism. What he is saying is this: "If I were a gentile and knew nothing of Jewish matters,

---

[3] Rom. 3:23
[4] Gal. 5:2
[5] Rom. 11:6
[6] Gal. 2:21
[7] Gal. 5:4

perhaps someone would say that, because I had no share in the Jewish plan and dispensation, because I did not know the power of circumcision, I reject it from the dogmas of the Church". This is why he added his name. He wished to remind them of what he had done in behalf of the Law. It is almost as if he were to say:

> I do this not through hatred of circumcision but in full knowledge of the truth. I, Paul, say this, that Paul who was circumcised on the eighth day, who am an Israelite by birth, a Hebrew of the Hebrews, of the tribe of Benjamin, a Pharisee according to the Law, who zealously persecuted the Church, who entered houses, dragged out men and women, and handed them over into custody. All this could persuade even those who are very stupid that I set down this law not through any hatred nor in ignorance of things Jewish but in full knowledge of the surpassing truth of Christ.

"I testify again to every man who receives circumcision that he is bound to keep the whole law".[8]

(3) Why did he not say: "I exhort", or "I command", or "I say"? Why did he say: "I testify?" So that he might, by this word, remind us of the future judgment. Where there are witnesses who testify, there also are judgments and sentences. He is frightening his hearer, then, by reminding him of the royal throne and by showing him that those very words will be his witness on that day when each man will give an account of what he has done, what he has said, and what he has heard. The Galatians heard those words in days gone by. Let those who are sick with the Galatians' disease hear them again today. If they are not present, let them hear through you the words that Paul exclaimed and said: "I testify again to every man who has himself circumcised, that he is bound to observe the whole Law".

(4) Do not tell me that circumcision is just a single command; it is that very command which imposes on you the entire yoke of the Law. When you subject yourself to the rule of the Law in one part, you must also obey its commands in all other things. If you do not fulfill it, you

---

[8] Gal. 5:3

must be punished and draw its curse upon yourself. When a sparrow has fallen into the hunter's net, even if only its foot is caught, all the rest of its body is caught as well. So, too, the man who fulfills a single commandment of the Law, be it circumcision or fasting, through that one commandment, has given the Law full power over himself; as long as he is willing, and if he is willing to obey a part of the Law, he cannot avoid obeying the whole Law.

(5) We do not say this in accusation of the Law. Heaven forbid! We say it because we wish to show forth the surpassing riches of the grace of Christ. For the Law is not contrary to Christ. How could it be, when he is the one who gave the Law, when the Law leads us to him? But we are forced to say all these things because of the untimely contentiousness of those who do not use the Law as they should. The ones who outrage the Law are those who bid us stand apart from it once and for all and come to Christ, and then tell us to hold fast to it again. The Law has profited our nature very much. I agree to that and would never deny it. But you Judaizers cling to it beyond the proper time and will not let us see how very useful it has been.

(6) It would be the greatest source of praise for a tutor if his young pupil no longer needed him to keep watch over his conduct because the lad had advanced to greater virtue. So, too, it would be the greatest praise for the Law that we no longer had need of its help. For the Law has brought that very thing to pass for us: it has prepared our soul to receive a greater philosophy.

(7) So it is that he who still sits at the feet of the Law and can see nothing greater than what is written therein derives no great profit from it. But I put the Law aside and ran to the loftier teachings of Christ; yet I could grant to the Law the greatest dignity because it made me such that I could go beyond the trivialities written therein and rise to the loftiness of the teaching which comes to us from Christ.

(8) The Law did profit our nature greatly, but only if it led us sincerely to Christ. If this be not the case, it did us harm by depriving us of the greater things because of our close attention to those which are less; it also hurt us by still keeping us in the countless wounds of our transgressions. Suppose there were two physicians, one weaker, the other stronger. If the weaker one applied medicines to the ulcers but could not free the sick man once and for all from the pain coming from his sores, then...

III

(1) "So if you are offering your gift at the altar, and there remember that your brother has something against you, leave your gift there before the altar and go; first be reconciled to your brother, and then come and offer your gift".[9] Christ did not say: "Submit your offering and then go away", but "Leave your gift there before the altar and go; first be reconciled to your brother."

(2) Nor did he do this only here but again in another place. If a man has an infidel wife, that is, a gentile, he is not forced to put her away. For St. Paul said: "If any brother has a wife who is an unbeliever, and she consents to live with him, he should not divorce her".[10] But if he has a wife who is a harlot and an adulteress, there is nothing to stop him from putting her away. For Christ said: "But I say to you that everyone who divorces his wife, except on the ground of unchastity, makes her an adulteress".[11] And so he is allowed to put her away because of immorality.

(3) Do you see God's loving-kindness and concern? He says: "If your wife be a gentile, do not put her away. But if she be a harlot, I do not stop you from doing so." What he means is this: "If she acts outrageously toward Me, do not put her away; if she outrages you, there is no one to stop you from putting her away." If God, then, showed us such honor, will we not deem him deserving of equal honor? Will we let him be outraged by our wives? Will we permit this even though we realize that the greatest punishment and vengeance will be stored up for us when we neglect the salvation of our wives?

(4) This is why he made you to be head of the wife. This is why Paul gave the order: "If there is anything they desire to know, let them ask their husbands at home",[12] so that you, like a teacher, a guardian, a patron, might urge her to godliness. Yet when the hour set for the services summons you to the church, you fail to rouse your wife from their sluggish indifference. But now that the devil summons your wives to the feast of the Trumpets and they turn a ready ear to this call, you do not restrain them. You let them entangle themselves in accusations of ungodliness, you let them be dragged off into licentious ways. For, as a rule, it

---

[9] Matt. 5:23-24
[10] 1 Cor. 7:12
[11] Matt. 5:32
[12] 1 Cor. 14:35

is the harlots, the effeminates, and the whole chorus from the theater who rush to that festival.

(5) And why do I speak of the immorality that goes on there? Are you not afraid that your wife may not come back from there after a demon has possessed her soul? Did you not hear in my previous discourse the argument which clearly proved to us that demons dwell in the very souls of the Jews and in places in which they gather? Tell me, then. How do you Judaizers have the boldness, after dancing with demons, to come back to the assembly of the apostles? After you have gone off and shared with those who shed the blood of Christ, how is it that you do not shudder to come back and share in his sacred banquet, to partake of his precious blood? Do you not shiver, are you not afraid when you commit such outrages? Have you so little respect for that very banquet?

(6) I have spoken these words to you. You will speak them to those Judaizers, and they to their wives. "Fortify one another." If a neophyte is sick with this disease, let him be kept outside the church doors. If the sick one be a believer and already initiated, let him be driven from the holy table. For not all sins need exhortation and counsel; some sins, of their very nature, demand cure by a quick and sharp excision. The wounds we can tolerate respond to more gentle cures; those which have festered and cannot be cured, those which are feeding on the rest of the body, need cauterization with a point of steel. So is it with sins. Some need long exhortation; others need sharp rebuke.

(7) This is why Paul did not enjoin us to exhort in every case but also to rebuke sharply: "Therefore rebuke them sharply".[13] Therefore, I will now rebuke them sharply, so that they may accuse themselves and feel shame for what they have done. Then they will never again be hurt by that sinful fast.

(8) So I shall put aside exhortation henceforth as I testify and exclaim: "If anyone has no love for the Lord, let him be accursed".[14] What greater evidence could there be that a man does not love our Lord than when he participates in the festival with those who slew Christ? It was not I who hurled the curse at them, but Paul. Rather, it was not Paul but

---

[13] Titus 1:13
[14] 1 Cor. 16:22

Christ, who spoke through him and said earlier: "You who would be justified by the law; you have fallen away from grace". [15]

(9) So speak these words to them, read aloud to them these texts.
Show all your zeal in saving them. When you have snatched them from
the devil's jaws, bring them to me on the day of the Jewish fast. Then,
after I have kept the rest of my promise to you, let us, with one accord
and with one voice, join our brothers in giving glory to God and the Father of our Lord Jesus Christ, for to Him is glory forever. Amen. [16]

---

[15] Gal. 5:4

[16] One version of Homily II includes a substantial amount of additional material
—although, the style is significantly different, which casts doubt on its authen-
ticity. And more to the point, there are very few references to Jews, which
again is suspicious. In any case, the extra wording is reproduced in the Appen-
dix, for those who may be interested.

HOMILY III

(1) Once again, a necessary and pressing need has interrupted the sequence of my recent discourses. I must put aside my struggles with the heretics for today and turn my attention to this necessary business. For I was ready to address your loving assembly again on the glory of the only-begotten Son of God, but the untimely obstinacy of those who wish to keep the first paschal fast forces me to devote my entire instruction to their cure. For the good shepherd does more than drive away the wolves; he also is most diligent in caring for his sheep who are sick. What does he gain if the flocks escape the jaws of the wild beasts but are then devoured by disease?

(2) The best general is the one who not only repels the siege engines of the enemy but first puts down rebellion within his own city. He knows well that there will be no victory over an outside foe as long as there is civil war within. Do you not know that there is no more destructive force than rebellion and obstinacy? Listen to the words of Christ: "If a kingdom is divided against itself, that kingdom cannot stand".[1] And yet, what is more powerful than a kingdom which possesses revenues of money, weapons, walls, fortresses, many soldiers, horses, and ten thousand other sources of strength?

(3) But even power as great as that is destroyed when it revolts against itself. Nothing produces weakness so effectively as contentiousness and strife; and nothing produces power and strength so effectively as love and concord. When Solomon grasped this truth, he said: "A brother helped is like a strong city".[2] Do you see the great strength which comes from concord? And do you see the great harm caused by contentiousness? A kingdom in revolt destroys itself. When two brothers are bound together and united into one, they are more unbreakable than any wall.

(4) I know that, by God's grace, most members of my flock are free from this disease and that the sickness involves only a few. But this is no reason for me to relax my care. If only ten, or five, or two, or even one

---

[1] Mark 3:24
[2] Prov. 18:19

were sick, he must not be neglected. If there is only one worthless outcast, still he is a brother, and Christ died for him. And Christ made great
account of the weak ones. He said: "But whoever causes one of these
little ones who believe in me to sin, it would be better for him to have a
great millstone fastened round his neck and to be drowned in the depth of
the sea".[3] And again: "Truly, I say to you, as you did it not to one of the
least of these, you did it not to me".[4] And again: "So it is not the will of
my Father who is in heaven that one of these little ones should perish".[5]

(5) Is it not absurd, when Christ shows such care for his little ones,
that we should refuse to care for them? Do not say: "He is one person."
Rather, you must say: "He is one, yes, but if we do not take care of him,
he will spread the disease to the rest." Paul said: "A little leaven leavens
the whole lump".[6] And our neglect of the little ones is what overturns and
destroys everything. Neglected wounds become serious, just as the serious
wounds would easily become minor if they receive the proper care.

(6) Moreover, the first thing I have to say to the Judaizers is that
nothing is worse than contentiousness and fighting, than tearing the
Church asunder and rending into many parts the robe which the robbers
did not dare to rip. Are not all the other heresies enough without our tearing each other apart? You must listen to Paul when he says: "But if you
bite and devour one another, take heed that you are not consumed by one
another".[7]

(7) Tell me this. Do you stray outside the flock and have you no fear
of the lion that prowls about outside the fold? "Your adversary the devil
prowls around like a roaring lion, seeking someone to devour".[8] Here
you see a shepherd's wisdom. He does not let the lion in among the
sheep for fear the lion may terrify the flock. Nor does he drive the lion
away from outside the fold. Why? So that he may gather all the sheep together inside the fold, because they are afraid of the wild beast outside. Do
you have no reverence and respect for your father? Then fear your foe. If
you separate yourself from the flock, your enemy will surely catch you.

---

[3] Matt. 18:6
[4] Matt. 25:45
[5] Matt. 18:14
[6] Gal. 5:9
[7] Gal. 5:15
[8] 1 Pet. 5:8

(8) Christ, too, could have driven the enemy away from the outside of the fold. But to make you sober and watchful, to make you constantly run to your mother for refuge, he permitted him to roar outside the fold. Why did he do this? So that when those within the fold hear his roar, they may take refuge together and be more closely bound to one another. Mothers who love their children also do this: when their children cry, they often threaten to throw them to the jaws of the wolves. Of course, they would not throw them to the wolves but they *say* they will, to stop the children from bothering them. Everything Christ did was done to keep us bound together and living at peace with one another.

II

(1) And so it was that Paul could have accused the Corinthians of many great crimes but he accused them of contentiousness before any other. He could have accused them of fornication, of pride, of taking their quarrels to the pagan courts, of banquets in the shrines of idols. He could have charged that the women did not veil their heads and that the men did. Over and above all this, he could have accused them of neglecting the poor, of the pride they took in their charismatic gifts, and in the matter of the resurrection of the body. But since, along with these, he could also find fault with them because of their dissensions and quarrels with one another, he passed over all the other crimes, and corrected their contentiousness first.

(2) If you suspect that I am making a nuisance of myself on this point, I shall clarify it from Paul's own words. He did give top priority to correcting the Corinthians' obstinacy and contentiousness. And he did this even though he could charge them with all those other crimes. Hear what he says about their fornication: "It is actually reported that there is immorality among you",[9] that they were puffed up and proud: "Some are arrogant, as though I were not coming to you".[10] Again, that they would plead their cases in the pagan courts: "When one of you has a grievance against a brother, does he dare go to law before the unrighteous instead of the saints?"[11] That they ate meat offered to idols: "You cannot partake

---

[9] 1 Cor. 5:1
[10] 1 Cor. 4:18-19
[11] 1 Cor. 6:1

of the table of the Lord and the table of demons".[12] Hear his words of reproach for the women who do not veil their heads and the men who do. "Any man who prays or prophesies with his head covered dishonors his head, but any woman who prays or prophesies with her head unveiled dishonors her head".[13] He showed that they neglected the poor when he said: "One is hungry and another is drunk".[14] And again: "Or do you despise the church of God and humiliate those who have nothing?"[15] When they were all jumping for the more important charismatic gifts and no one was satisfied with the less important, he said: "Are all apostles? Are all prophets?"[16] We can conclude that they were raising doubts about the resurrection because he says: "But someone will ask, 'How are the dead raised? With what kind of body do they come?'"[17]

(3) Although he could make so many accusations, his first charge against the Corinthians was dissension and contentiousness. At the very beginning of his letter, he said: "I appeal to you, brethren, by the name of our Lord Jesus Christ, that all of you agree and that there be no dissensions among you".[18] For he knew, he knew clearly, that this problem was more urgent than the others. If the fornicator, or the braggart. or a man in the grip of any other vice comes frequently to the church, he will quickly draw profit from the instruction, thrust aside his sin, and return to health.

(4) But when a man has broken away from this assembly, when he has withdrawn from the instruction of the fathers, when he has fled from the physician's clinic, even if he appears to be in good health, he will soon fall sick. The best physicians first quench the fires of fever and then cure the wounds and fractures. That is what Paul did. He first removed the dissension and then cured their wounds limb by limb. And so he spoke of dissension before the other sins, so that the Corinthians would not stand apart in strife, so that they would not choose the leaders whom they should follow, so that they would not divide up the body of Christ into many parts.

---

[12] 1 Cor. 10:21
[13] 1 Cor. 11:4-5
[14] 1 Cor. 11:21
[15] 1 Cor. 11:22
[16] 1 Cor. 12:29
[17] 1 Cor. 15:35
[18] 1 Cor. 1:10

(5) But he was talking not only to the Corinthians; he was also speaking to those who would come after them and suffer from the same Corinthian disease. I would be glad to ask those of us who are sick with this illness: What is the Pasch; what is Lent? What belongs to the Jews; what belongs to us? Why does their Pasch come once each year; why do we celebrate ours each time we gather to celebrate the mysteries? What does the feast of unleavened bread mean? And I would like to ask them many more questions which contribute to understanding this subject.

(6) If I were to ask them, you would then clearly know how untimely the contentiousness of these men is. They cannot explain what they do. But they refuse to ask anybody, just as if they were wiser than anyone else. They deserve the strongest condemnation because they do not have the answers themselves, but they refuse to follow those who have been appointed to lead them. They have simply risked all they have on this silly practice and are throwing themselves head-first down into the depths of danger.

III

(1) When I have this to say against them, what argument of theirs will seem clever? They ask: "Did you not observe this fast before?" It is not your place to say this to me, but I would be justified in telling you that we, too, fasted at this time in earlier days, but still we put more importance on peace than on the observance of dates. And I say to you what Paul said to the Galatians: "Become as I am, for I also have become as you are".[19] What does this mean? He was urging them to renounce circumcision, to scorn the Sabbath, the feast days, and all the other observances of the Law. When he saw they were frightened and afraid that they might be subjected to chastisement and punishment for their transgression, he gave them courage by the example of his own actions when he said, "Become like me, because I also have become like you".

(2) For, he said, I did not come from the Gentiles, did I? I was not without experience of the Jewish way of life under the Law and the punishment set for those who transgress it, was I? "A Hebrew born of Hebrews; as to the law a Pharisee, as to zeal a persecutor of the church, as to righteousness under the law blameless. But whatever gain I had, I count-

---

[19] Gal. 4:12

ed as loss for the sake of Christ".[20] That is, once and for all I stood aloof from them. Therefore, become like me, for I, too, was as you are.

(3) But why do I speak on my own account? Three hundred Fathers or even more gathered together in the land of Bithynia and ordained this by law; yet you disdain their decrees. You must choose one of two courses: Either you charge them with *ignorance* for their want of exact knowledge on this matter, or you charge them with *cowardice* because they were not ignorant, but played the hypocrite and betrayed the truth. When you do not abide by what they decreed, this is exactly the choice you must make. But all the events of the Council make it clear that they showed great wisdom and courage at that time. The article of faith they set forth at the Council show how wise they were, because they blocked up the mouths of heretics and, like an impregnable wall, they repelled the treachery of every hostile attack. They proved their courage during the war waged on the Churches and the persecution which had but lately come to an end.

(4) Like champions in battle who have set up many memorials of victory and have suffered many wounds, so, too, these champions of the Churches, who could count the many tortures they had endured for their confession of the faith, came together from every side, bearing on their bodies the marks of Christ's wounds. Some could tell of their hardships in the mines, others of the confiscation of all their possessions, and still others of starvation and continuous floggings. Some could show where the flesh had been torn from their ribs, some where their backs had been broken, some where their eyes had been dug out, and still others where they had lost some other part of their bodies for the sake of Christ. At that time, the whole synodal gathering, welded together from these champions, along with their definition of what Christians must believe, also passed a decree that they celebrate the paschal feast in harmony together. They refused to betray their faith in those most difficult times [of persecution]; would they sink to pretense and deceit on the question of the Easter observance?

(5) Look what you do when you condemn Fathers so great, so courageous, so wise. If the Pharisee lost all the blessings he possessed because he condemned the tavern keeper, what excuse will you have, what

---

[20] Phil. 3:5-7

defense will you make for rising up against these great teachers beloved of God, especially since your attack is so unjust and irrational? Did you not hear Christ himself say: "For where two or three are gathered in my name, there am I in the midst of them"?[21] But if Christ is in their midst where two or three are gathered together, was not his presence all the more pervasive among the more than 300 Fathers at Nicaea? Christ was present there, it was Christ who formulated and passed the laws. Yet you condemn not only the Council Fathers but the whole world which approved their judgment.

(6) Do you consider that the Jews are wiser than the Fathers who came from everywhere in the world? How can you do that when the Jews have been driven from their ancestral commonwealth and way of life, and have no sacred festival to celebrate? I hear many say that the Pasch and the feast of unleavened bread are one. But there is no feast of unleavened bread among them, nor is there a Pasch. Why is there no feast of unleavened bread among them? Hear the words of the Lawgiver: "You may not offer the Passover sacrifice within any of your towns which the Lord your God gives you; but at the place which the Lord your God will choose, to make his name dwell in it".[22] And Moses was here speaking of Jerusalem.

(7) Do you see how God confined the festival to one city, and later destroyed the city so that, even if it was against their wills, he might lead them away from that way of life? Surely, it is clear to everyone that God foresaw what would come to pass. Why, then, did he bring them together to that land from all over the world if he foresaw that their city would be destroyed? Is it not very obvious that he did this because he wished to bring their ritual to an end? God did bring the ritual to an end, but you go along with the Jews, of whom the prophet said: "Who is blind but my servant, or deaf as my messenger whom I send?"[23]

(8) And against whom did they show their want of sense and feeling? Was it not against the apostles, the prophets, and their teachers? Why must I mention teachers and prophets when they slaughtered their own children? For they did sacrifice their sons and daughters to demons. When they ignored the voice of nature, were they going to observe the

---

[21] Matt. 18:20
[22] Deut. 16:5-6
[23] Isa. 42:19

festival days? Tell me this. Did they not trample kinship under foot, did they not forget their children, did they not forget the very God who created them? Moses said: "You were unmindful of the Rock that begot you, and you forgot the God who gave you birth".[24] Were they going to keep the festivals after they had forsaken God? Who could say that?

(9) Christ did keep the Pasch with them. Yet he did not do so with the idea that we should keep the Pasch with them. He did so that he might bring the reality to what foreshadowed the reality. He also submitted to circumcision, kept the Sabbath, observed the festival days, and ate the unleavened bread. But He did all these things in Jerusalem. However, we are subject to none of these things, and on this Paul spoke out loud and clear: "If you receive circumcision, Christ will be of no advantage to you".[25] And again, speaking of the feast of unleavened bread, he said: "Let us, therefore, celebrate the festival, not with the old leaven, the leaven of malice and evil, but with the unleavened bread of sincerity and truth".[26] For our unleavened bread is not a mixed flour but an uncorrupted and virtuous way of life.

IV

(1) Why did Christ keep the Pasch at that time? The old Pasch was a type of the Pasch to come, and the reality had to supplant the type. So Christ first showed the foreshadowing and then brought the reality to the banquet table. Once the reality has come, the type which foreshadowed it is henceforth lost in its own shadow and no longer fills the need. So do not keep pleading this excuse, but show me that Christ did command us to observe the old Pasch. I am showing you quite the opposite. I am showing you that Christ not only did not command us to keep the festival days but even freed us from the obligation to do so.

(2) Hear what Paul had to say. And when I speak of Paul, I mean Christ; for it is Christ who moved Paul's soul to speak. What, then, did Paul say? "You observe days, and months, and seasons, and years! I am afraid I have labored over you in vain".[27] And again: "For as often as you eat this bread and drink the cup, you proclaim the Lord's death until he

---

[24] Deut. 32:18
[25] Gal. 5:2
[26] 1 Cor. 5:8
[27] Gal. 4:10-11

comes".[28] When he said: "As often as," Paul gave the right and power to decide this to those who approach the mysteries, and freed them from any obligation to observe the festival days.

(3) Now our Pasch and Lent are not one and the same thing: the Pasch is one thing, Lent another. Lent comes once each year; our Pasch is celebrated three times each week, sometimes even four times, or rather as often as we wish. For the Pasch is not a fast but the offering and sacrifice which is celebrated at each religions service That you may know that this is true, listen to Paul when he says: "For Christ, our paschal lamb, has been sacrificed,"[29] and again: "As often as you shall eat this bread and drink the cup, you proclaim the death of the Lord."

(4) So as often as you approach the sacrificial banquet with a clean conscience, you celebrate the Pasch. You celebrate it not when you fast but when you share in that sacrifice. "For as often as you shall eat this bread and drink this cup, you proclaim the death of the Lord." Our Pasch is the proclamation of the Lord's death. The sacrifice which we offer today, that which was offered yesterday, and each day's sacrifice is alike and the same as the sacrifice offered on that Sabbath day; the sacrifice offered on that Sabbath is no more solemn than today's, nor is today's of less value than that; they are one and the same, alike filled with awe and salvation.

(5) Why, then, do we fast for 40 days? In the past, and especially at the time when Christ entrusted to us these sacred mysteries, many a man approached the sacrificial banquet without thought or preparation. Since the Fathers realized that it was harmful for a person to approach the mysteries in this heedless fashion, they came together and marked out 40 days for people to fast, pray, and gather together to hear the word of God. Their purpose was that we might all scrupulously purify ourselves during this time by our prayers. almsgiving, fasting, vigils tears, confessions, and all the other pious practices, so that we might approach the mysteries with our consciences made as clean as we could make them.

(6) And they did well when they came to our aid and established for us the practice of this Lenten fast. This is clear because, if we keep shouting and proclaiming a fast the whole year through, no one listens to what

---

[28] 1 Cor. 11:26
[29] 1 Cor. 5:7

we say. But as soon as the season of Lent draws near, even the laziest of men rouses himself, even though no one counsels or advises him. Why? He gets advice and counsel from the season of Lent.

(7) So if a Jew or pagan ask you why you are fasting, do not tell him that it is because of the Pasch or because of the mystery of the cross. If you tell him that, you give him an ample grip upon you. Tell him we fast *because of our sins* and because we are going to *approach the mysteries*. The Pasch is not a reason for fasting or grief; it is a reason for cheerfulness and joy. The cross has taken away sin; it was an expiation for the world, a reconciliation for the ancient enmity. It opened the gates of heaven, changed those who hated into friends; it took our human nature, led it up to heaven, and seated it at the right hand of God's throne. And it brought to us ten thousand other blessings.

(8) There is no need, then, to grieve or be downcast: We must rejoice and glory in all these things. This is why Paul said: "But far be it from me to glory except in the cross of our Lord Jesus Christ".[30] And again: "But God shows his love for us in that while we were yet sinners Christ died for us".[31] John put it like this: "God so loved the world". Tell me, how did God love the world? John passed over all the other signs of God's love and put the cross in first place. For after he said: "For God so loved the world that he gave his only Son,"[32] that he be crucified, "that whoever believes in him should not perish but have eternal life".[33] If, then, the cross is the basis and boast of love, let us not say that it is a cause for grief. Heaven forbid that we grieve because of the cross. We grieve for our sins, and this is why we fast.

V

(1) Although the neophyte keeps the fast each year, he does not celebrate the Pasch since he does not share in the sacrifice. But even though a man is not observing the Lenten fast, he does celebrate the Pasch as long as he comes to the altar with a clean conscience and shares in the sacrifice— whether it be today, tomorrow, or any day whatsoever. The best time to

---

[30] Gal. 6:14
[31] Rom. 5:8
[32] John 3:16
[33] John 3:16

approach the mysteries is determined by the purity of a man's conscience and not by his observance of suitable seasons.

(2) Yet we do just the opposite. We fail to cleanse our conscience and, even though we are burdened with ten thousand sins, we consider that we have celebrated the Pasch as long as we approach the mysteries on that feast day. But this is certainly not the case. If you approach the altar on the very day of the Sabbath and your conscience be bad, you fail to share in the mysteries and you leave without celebrating the Pasch. But if you wash away your sins and share in the mysteries today, you do celebrate the Pasch in precisely the proper way.

(3) Therefore you must safeguard this exactness and vigor of spirit, not in the observance of the proper times but in your approach to the altar. Now you would elect to endure all things rather than change this practice. So, too, you must disdain it and choose to do or suffer anything so as not to approach the mysteries when you are burdened with sins.

(4) Be sure that God takes no account of such observance of special seasons. Hear him as he passes judgment on those at his right hand: "For I was hungry and you gave me food, I was thirsty and you gave me drink, I was a stranger and you welcomed me, I was naked and you clothed me".[34] But he charged with quite different conduct those on his left hand. At another time he brought forward another man in a parable and castigated him because He remembered the evil the man had done. For he said: "You wicked servant! I forgave you all that debt because you besought me; and should not you have had mercy on your fellow servant, as I had mercy on you?"[35] Again, when the virgins had no oil in their lamps, he locked them out of the bride chamber. And he cast out another man who came into the feast without a wedding garment because this man was garbed in filthy clothes and was wearing the cloak of his fornication and uncleanness. But no one was ever punished or accused because he observed the Pasch in this or that month.

(5) But why speak of ourselves since we have been set free from all such necessity? We are citizens of a city above in heaven, where there are no months, no sun, no moon, no circle of seasons. If you wish to give exact attention to the matter, you will see that, even among the Jews, lit-

---

[34] Matt. 25:35-40
[35] Matt. 18:32-33

tle account was made of the season of the Pasch, but they cared greatly about the place for it, namely, Jerusalem. Some men came up to Moses and said to him: "We are unclean through touching the dead body of a man; why are we kept from offering the Lord's offering at its appointed time among the people of Israel?" He said to them: "Wait, that I may hear what the Lord will command concerning you".[36] Then, after he reported it, he brought back the law which says: "If any man of you or of your descendants is unclean through touching a dead body, or is afar off on a journey, he shall still keep the Passover to the Lord. In the second month on the fourteenth day in the evening, they shall keep it".[37]

(6) And so is not the observance of the time annulled among the Jews so that the Pasch may be observed in Jerusalem? Will you not show greater concern for the harmony of the Church than for the season? So that you may seem to be observing the proper days, will you outrage the common Mother of us all and will you cut asunder the Holy Synod? How could you deserve pardon when you choose to commit sins so enormous for no good reason?

(7) But why must I speak of the Jews? No matter how eagerly and earnestly we wish it, it is not altogether possible for us to observe that day on which He was crucified. This will make it clear. Let us suppose the Jews had not sinned, that they were not hard of heart, nor senseless, nor indifferent, nor despisers; suppose they had not fallen from their ancestral way of life but were still carefully observing it. Even if this was the case, we could not, by following in their footsteps, put our finger on the very day on which He was crucified and fulfilled the Pasch. Let me tell how this is the case. When He was crucified, it was the first day of the feast of unleavened bread and the day of preparation.

(8) But it is not possible for both of these to fall always on the same day. This year the first day of the feast of unleavened bread falls on Sunday, and the fast must still last for a whole week; according to this, after Passiontide, after the cross and resurrection have come and gone, we are still fasting. And it has often happened that, after the cross and resurrection, our fast is still being observed because the week is not yet over. This is why no observance of the exact time is possible.

---

[36] Num. 9:7-8
[37] Num. 9:10-11

VI

(1) Let us not quarrel, let us not say: "After fasting these many years, am I to change now?" Change for that very reason. Since you have been so long severed from the Church, come back now to your Mother. No one says: "After I lived as her enemy so long a time, I am ashamed to be reconciled now." You have grounds for shame if you do not change for the better but persist in your untimely contentiousness. That is what destroyed the Jews. While they always kept looking for the old customs and life, these were stripped from them and they turned to impiety.

(2) But why do I speak of fasting and the observance of special days? Paul continued to observe the Law and to endure many a toil; he patiently put up with many journeys and hardships; he surpassed all his contemporaries in the exact observance of that way of life. But after he achieved the heights of that life and came to realize that he was doing all this for his own hurt and destruction, he immediately changed. He did not say to himself: "What is this? Am I to lose the reward for this great zeal of mine? Am I to waste all this work?" Rather he was the quicker to change for the very reason that he might continue to suffer that loss. He scorned justification by the Law so that he might receive the justification of faith. And so he loudly proclaimed: "But whatever gain I had, I counted as loss for the sake of Christ".[38] And Christ said: "So if you are offering your gift at the altar, and there remember that your brother has something against you, leave your gift there before the altar and go; first be reconciled to your brother, and then come and offer your gift".[39]

(3) What do you mean? If your brother has something against you, Christ does not permit you to offer your sacrifice until you are reconciled to your brother. When you have the whole Church and so many Fathers against you, do you have the hardihood to dare to approach the divine mysteries before you put aside that unseemly enmity? Since this is the way you feel, how could you celebrate the Pasch?

(4) I say this not only to those who are sick but also to you who are in good health. When you who are well see how many are sick, you will show them great care and kindness, you will pick them out, gather them together, and bring them back to their Mother. Whatever they say against

---

[38] Phil. 3:7
[39] Matt. 5:23-24

us, however they jump at us, no matter what else they do to us, we must not grow weary and stop until we win them back. For there is nothing comparable to peace and harmony.

(5) It is for this reason that, when the Father enters the church, he does not mount to this chair until he has prayed for all of you; when he rises from this chair, he does not begin his instruction until he has first given the peace to all. And when the priests are going to give the blessing, they first pray for peace for you and then begin the blessing.

(6) And when the deacon bids you to pray all together, he also enjoins you in his prayer to ask for the Angel of Peace, and that everything which concerns you be blessed with peace. As he dismisses you from the assembly, he petitions [peace] for you and says: "Go in peace." And without this peace, it is altogether impossible for us to say or do anything. For peace is our nurse and mother; she is very careful to cherish us and foster us. I am not speaking of what is merely called by the name of peace, nor of the peace which comes from sharing meals together, but of the peace which accords with God, the peace which comes from the harmony sent by the Spirit. Many are now tearing this peace asunder by destroying us and exalting the Jews. These men consider the Jews as more trustworthy teachers than their own Fathers; they believe the account of Christ's passion and death which is given by those who slew Him. What could be more unreasonable than this?

(7) Do you not see that their Passover is the type, while our Pasch is the truth? Look at the tremendous difference between them. The Passover prevented bodily death: whereas the Pasch quelled God's anger against the whole world; the Passover of old freed the Jews from Egypt, while the Pasch has set us free from idolatry; the Passover drowned the Pharaoh, but the Pasch drowned the devil; after the Passover came Palestine, but after the Pasch will come heaven.

(8) Why, then, do you sit beside a lamp after the sun has appeared? Why do you wish to nourish yourself on milk when solid food is being given to you? You were nourished with milk so that you might not remain satisfied with milk; the lamp shone for you that it might guide you and lead you by the hand into the light of the sun. Now that the era of more perfect things has come, let us not run back to the former times, let us not observe the days and seasons and years; rather, let us everywhere

be careful to follow the Church by paying heed to charity and peace before all things.

(9) Suppose the Church were to be tripped up and fall. The accurate
computation of dates would not succeed in making her slip as much as
this division and schism would deserve the blame. But I make no account
of the exact date, since God makes no account of it, as I proved when I
devoted many discourses to this subject. But the one thing I seek is that
we do all things in peace and concord. If we do so, you will not stay
home and get drunk while we are fasting with the rest of the people, and
the priests are praying together for the whole world.

(10) Note well that this is of the devil's doing and that it is not a
single sin, nor two, nor three, but far more than three. It cuts you off from
the flock, it makes you ready to hold so many Fathers in scorn, it hurls
you into contentiousness, it thrusts you over to the Jews, and furthermore
it makes you a scandal both to your own family and to strangers. How
can we blame the Jews for waiting for you in their houses when it is you
who go running to them?

(11) These sins are not the only problem. During those days of the
fast, great harm could come to you from your failure to take advantage of
the Scripture readings, the religious meetings in the church, the blessing,
and the prayers said in common. Great harm could come to you while
you and your bad conscience are spending tiffs whole time in fear and
dread that, like some foreigner or stranger, you may be caught ill your
sinful act. And during all this time, in common with the Church, you
should be discharging all your religious duties in a spirit of confidence,
pleasure, good cheer, and full freedom.

(12) The Church does not recognize the exact observance of dates.
In the beginning, the Fathers decided to come together from widely separated places and to fix the Easter date; the Church paid respect to the harmony of their thinking, loved their oneness of mind, and accepted the date
they enjoined. My earlier remarks have proved adequately that it is impossible for us or you or any other man to arrive at the exact date of the Lord's
day. So let us stop fighting with shadows, let us stop hurting ourselves in
the big things while we are indulging our rivalry over the small.

(13) Fasting at this or that time is not a matter for blame. But to rend
asunder the Church, to be ready for rivalry, to create dissension, to rob
oneself continuously of the benefits of religious meetings—these are un-

pardonable, these do demand an accounting, these do deserve serious punishment.

(14) I could have said much more than this. What I have said is enough for those who heed me; those who fail to heed my words will not be helped even if I should have much more to say. So let me finish my discourse at this point, and let us all pray together that our brothers come back to us. Let us pray that they cling fondly to peace and stand apart from untimely rivalry. Let us pray that they scorn this sluggish spirit of theirs and find a great and lofty understanding. Let us pray that they be set free from this observance of days so that all of us, with one heart and with one voice, may give glory to God and the Father of our Lord Jesus Christ, to whom be glory and power now and forever, world without end. Amen.

HOMILY IV

(1) Again the Jews, the most miserable and wretched of all men, are going to fast, and again we must make secure the flock of Christ. As long as no wild beast disturbs the flock, shepherds, as they stretch out under an oak or pine tree and play their flutes, let their sheep go off to graze with full freedom. But when the shepherds feel that the wolves will raid, they are quick to throw down the flute and pick up their slingshots; they cast aside the pipe of reeds and arm themselves with clubs and stones. They take their stand in front of the flock, raise a loud and piercing shout, and oftentimes the sound of their shout drives the wolf away before he strikes.

(2) I, too, in the past, frolicked about in explicating the Scriptures, as if I were sporting in some meadow; I took no part in polemics because there was no one causing me concern. But today the Jews, who are more dangerous than any wolves, are bent on surrounding my sheep; so I must spar with them and fight with them so that no sheep of mine may fall victim to those wolves.

(3) That fast will not be upon us for ten days or more. But do not be surprised that, from today on, I am taking up my tools and building a fence around your souls. This is what the hard-working farmer does. When he has a rushing stream nearby which may wash away the fields he has tilled, he does not wait for winter. Long beforehand, he fences in the banks, builds up dikes, digs ditches, and makes every preparation against the flood. While the stream runs quietly and is low in its bed, it is a simpler matter to restrain it; when it has become swollen and is swept along with a violent rush of waters, it is no longer so simple to oppose the flood. And so it is that, long beforehand, the farmer anticipates the surge of the torrent and contrives by every means to keep his fields secure in every way.

(4) As well as farmers, every soldier, sailor, and reaper makes it a practice to prepare ahead. Before the hour of battle, the soldier cleans off his breastplate, examines his shield, makes ready the bridle and bit, feeds and cares for his horse, and sees to it that he is well-prepared in every way. Before the sailor launches his ship into the harbor's waters, he prepares the keel, repairs the sides, hews and shapes the oars, stitches to-

gether the sails, and makes ready all the other equipment of his ship. Many days before the harvest, the reaper sharpens his sickle, gets ready the threshing-floor, his oxen, his wagon, and everything else which may help him in the harvest. Indeed, you can see men everywhere making preparations for their business beforehand so that, when the time does come, it is an easy matter for them to carry on their enterprise.

(5) I am following the example of these men. Many days beforehand I am making your souls secure by exhorting you to flee from that accursed and unlawful fast. Do not tell me that the Jews are fasting; *prove to me* that it is God's will that they fast. If it be not God's will, then their fasting is more unlawful than any drunkenness? For we must not only look at what they do but we must also seek out the reason why they do it.

(6) What is done in accordance with God's will is the best of all things, even if it seems to be bad. What is done contrary to God's will and decree is the worst and most unlawful of all things—even if men judge that it is very good. Suppose someone slays another in accordance with God's will. This slaying is better than any loving-kindness. Let someone spare another and show him great love and kindness against God's decree. To spare the other's life would be more unholy than any slaying. For it is God's will and not the nature of things that makes the same actions good or bad.

II

(1) Listen to me so that you may learn that this is true. Ahab once captured a king of Syria and, contrary to God's decree, saved his life. He had the Syrian king enjoy a seat by his side and sent him off with great honor. About that time, a prophet came to his companion and

> said to his fellow at the command of the Lord, "Strike me, I pray." But the man refused to strike him. Then he said to him, "Because you have not obeyed the voice of the Lord, behold, as soon as you have gone from me, a lion shall kill you." And as soon as he had departed from him, a lion met him and killed him. Then he found another man, and said, "Strike me, I pray." And the man struck him, smiting and wounding him. So the prophet departed, and waited for the

king by the way, disguising himself with a bandage over his eyes.[1]

(2) What greater paradox than this could there be? The man who struck the prophet was saved; the one who spared the prophet was punished. Why? That you may learn that, when God commands, you must not question too much the nature of the action; you have only to obey. So that the first man might not spare him out of reverence, the prophet did not simply say: "Strike me" but said: "Strike me in the word of God." That is, God commands it; seek no further. It is the King who ordains it; reverence the rank of him who commands and with all eagerness heed his word. But the man lacked the courage to strike him and, on this account, he paid the ultimate penalty. But by the punishment he subsequently suffered, he encourages us to yield and obey God's every command.

(3) But after the second man had struck and wounded him, the prophet bound his own head with a bandage, covered his eyes, and disguised himself. Why did he do this? He was going to accuse the king and condemn him for saving the life of the king of the Syrians. Now, Ahab was an impious man and always a foe to the prophets. The prophet did not wish Ahab to recognize him and then drive him from his sight; if the king drove him away, he would not hear the prophet's words of correction. So the prophet concealed his face and any statement of his business in the hope that this would give him the advantage when he did speak and that he might get the king to agree to the terms he wanted.

(4)

> And as the king passed, he cried to the king and said, "Your servant went out into the midst of the battle; and behold, a soldier turned and brought a man to me, and said, 'Keep this man; if by any means he be missing, your life shall be for his life, or else you shall pay a talent of silver.' And as your servant was busy here and there, he was gone." The king of Israel said to him, "So shall your judgment be; you yourself have decided it." Then he made haste to take the bandage away from his eyes; and the king of Israel recognized him as one of the prophets. And he said to him, "Thus

---

[1] 1 Kings 20:35-39

says the Lord, 'Because you have let go out of your hand the
man whom I had devoted to destruction, therefore your life
shall go for his life, and your people for his people'."[2]

(5) Do you see how not only God but men make this kind of judgment because both God and men heed the end and the causes rather than
the nature of what is done? Certainly even the king said to him: "So shall
your judgment be; you yourself have decided it." You are a murderer, he
said, because you let an enemy go. The prophet put on the bandage and
presented the case as if it were not the king but somebody else on trial, so
that the king might pass the proper sentence. And, in fact, this did happen. For after the king condemned him, the prophet tore off the bandage
and said: "Because you have let go out of your hand the man whom I had
devoted to destruction, therefore your life shall go for his life, and your
people for his people."

(6) Did you see what a penalty the king paid for his act of kindness?
And what punishment he endured in return for his untimely sparing of
his foe? The one who spared a life is punished; another, who slew a man,
was held in esteem. Phinehas certainly slew two people in a single moment of time—a man and his wife; and after he slew them, he was given
the honor of the priesthood.[3] His act of bloodshed did not defile his
hands; it even made them cleaner.

(7) So you see that he who struck the prophet goes free, while he
who refused to strike him perishes; you see that he who spared a man's
life is punished, while he who refused to spare a life is held in esteem.
Therefore, always look into the decrees of God before you consider the
nature of your own actions. Whenever you find something which accords
with His decree, approve that—and only that.

III

(1) Let us examine the matter of fasting and apply this rule to it. Suppose
we should not apply this rule but merely take the act of fasting and consider it with no reference to anything else. The result will be great tumult
and confusion. It is true that highwaymen, grave-robbers, and sorcerers

---

[2] 1 Kings 20:39-42
[3] Num 25:7-13

have their sides torn to pieces; it is also true that the martyrs undergo this same suffering. What is done is the same, but the purpose and reason why it is done is different. And so it is that there is a great difference between the criminals and martyrs.

(2) In these cases, we not only consider the torture but we first look for the intention and the reasons why the torture is inflicted. And this is why we love the martyrs—not because they are tortured but because they are tortured for the sake of Christ. But we turn our backs on the robbers-not because they are being punished but because they are being punished for their wickedness.

(3) So, too, in the matter of fasting, you must pass a judgment. If you see people fasting for the sake of God, approve what they do; if you see that they do this against God's will, turn your back on them and hate them more than you do those who drink, revel, and carouse. And in the case of this fasting, we must inquire not only into the reason for fasting but we must consider also the place and the time.

(4) But before I draw up my battleline against the Jews, I will be glad to talk to those who are members of our own body, those who seem to belong to our ranks although they observe the Jewish rites and make every effort to defend them. Because they do this, as I see it, they deserve a stronger condemnation than any Jew. Not only the wise and intelligent but even those with little reason and understanding would agree with me in this. I need no clever arguments, no rhetorical devices, no prolix periodic sentences to prove this. It is enough to ask them a few simple questions and then trap them by their answers.

(5) What, then, are the questions? I will ask each one who is sick with this disease: Are you a Christian? Why, then, this zeal for Jewish practices? Are you a Jew? Why then, are you making trouble for the Church? Does not a Persian side with the Persians? Is not a barbarian eager for what concerns the barbarians? Will a man who lives in the Roman Empire not follow our laws and way of life? Tell me this. If ever anyone living among us is caught in collusion siding with the barbarians, is he not immediately punished? He is given neither hearing nor examination, even if he has ten thousand arguments in his own defense. If ever anyone living among the barbarians is clearly following Roman custom and law, again, will he not suffer the same punishment? How, then, do you expect to be saved by defecting to that unlawful way of life?

(6) The difference between the Jews and us in not a small one, is it? Is the dispute between us over ordinary, everyday matters, so that you think the two religions are really one and the same? Why are you mixing what cannot be mixed? They crucified the Christ whom you adore as God. Do you see how great the difference is? How is it, then, that you keep running to those who slew Christ when you say that you worship him whom they crucified? You do not think, do you, that I am the one who brings up the law on which these charges are based, nor that I make up the form which the accusation takes? Does not the Scripture treat the Jews in this way?

(7) Hear what Jeremiah says against those same Jews: "For cross to the coasts of Cyprus and see, or send to Kedar and examine with care; see if there has been such a thing".[4] What things? "Has a nation changed its gods, even though they are no gods? But my people have changed their glory for that which does not profit".[5] He did not say: "You have changed your God," but, "your glory." What he means is this. Those who worship idols and serve demons are so unshaken in their errors that they choose not to abandon them nor desert them for the truth. But you, who worship the true God, have cast aside the religion of your fathers and have gone over to strange ways of worship. You did not show the same firmness in regard to the truth that they did in regard to their error. That is why Jeremiah says: "See if there has been such a thing. Has a nation changed its gods, even though they are no gods? But my people have changed their glory for that which does not profit." He did not say: "You have changed your God," for God does not change. But he did say: "You have changed your glory." You did no harm to me, God says, because no harm has come to me. But you did dishonor yourselves. You did not make my glory less, but you did diminish your own.

(8) Let me also say this to those who are our own—if I must call our own those who side with the Jews. Go to the synagogues and see if the Jews have changed their fast; see if they kept the pre-Paschal fast with us; see if they have taken food on that day. But theirs is not a fast; it is a transgression of the law, it is a sin, it is trespassing. Yet they did not

---

[4] Jer. 2:10
[5] Jer. 2:11

change. But you did change your glory and from it you will derive no profit; you did go over to their rites.

(9) Did the Jews ever observe our pre-Paschal fast? Did they ever join us in keeping the feast of the martyrs? Did they ever share with us the day of the Epiphanies? They do not run to the truth, but you rush to transgression. I call it 'a transgression' because their observances do not occur at the proper time. Once there was a proper time when they had to follow those observances, but now there is not. That is why what was once according to the Law is now opposed to it.

IV

(1) Let me say what Elijah said against the Jews. He saw the unholy life the Jews were living: at one time they paid heed to God, at another they worshipped idols. So he spoke some such words as these: "How long will you go limping with two different opinions? If the Lord is God, follow him; but if Ba'al, then follow him".[6] Let me, too, now say this against these Judaizing Christians. If you judge that Judaism is the true religion, why are you causing trouble to the Church? But if Christianity is the true faith, as it really is, stay in it and follow it. Tell me this: Do you share with us in the mysteries, do you worship Christ as a Christian, do you ask him for blessings…and do you then celebrate the festival with his foes? With what purpose, then, do you come to the church?

(2) I have said enough against those who say they are on our side but are eager to follow the Jewish rites. Since it is against the Jews that I wish to draw up my battle line, let me extend my instruction further. Let me show that, by fasting now, the Jews dishonor the law and trample underfoot God's commands because they are always doing everything contrary to his decrees. When God wished them to fast, they got fat and flabby; when God does not wish them to fast, they get obstinate and do fast; when he wished them to offer sacrifices. they rushed off to idols; when he does not wish them to celebrate the feast days, they are all eager to observe them.

(3) This is why Stephen said to them: "You always resist the Holy Spirit".[7] This is the one thing, he says, in which you show your zeal: in

---

[6] 1 Kings 18:21
[7] Acts 7:51

doing the opposite to what God has commanded. And they are still doing that today. What makes this clear? The Law itself. In the case of the Jewish festivals, the Law demanded observance not only of the time but also the place. In speaking about this feast of the Passover, the Law says to them something such as this: "You may not offer the passover sacrifice within any of your towns which the Lord your God gives you".[8] The Law bids them keep the feast on the 14th day of the first month and in the city of Jerusalem. The Law also narrowed down the time and place for the observance of Pentecost, when it commanded them to celebrate the feast after seven weeks; and again, when it stated: "but at the place which the Lord your God will choose, to make his name dwell in it".[9] So also the Law fixed the feast of Tabernacles.

(4) Now let us see which of the two, time or place, is more necessary, even though neither the one nor the other has the power to save. Must we scorn the place but observe the time? Or should we scorn the time and keep the place? What I mean is something such as this. The Law commanded that the Passover be held in the first month and in Jerusalem, at a prescribed time and in a prescribed place. Let us suppose that there are two men keeping the Passover. Suppose one of them neglects the place but observes the time; suppose the other observes the place but neglects the time. Let the one who observes the time but neglects the place celebrate the Passover in the first month, but far away from Jerusalem; and let the one who observes the place but neglects the time celebrate the feast in Jerusalem but in the second month instead of the first.

(5) Next, let us see which of these two is charged and accused, and which receives approval and esteem. Will it be the one who transgressed in the matter of time but observed the place, or the one who neglected the place but observed the time? If the man who transgressed about the time so as to celebrate the feast in Jerusalem clearly deserves esteem, but the one who observed the time while neglecting the place deserves to be charged and accused for his impious action, it is quite obvious that those who do not keep the Passover in the proper place are transgressing the Law, even if they maintain a thousand times over that they are observing the proper time.

---

[8] Deut. 16:5
[9] Deut. 16:6

(6) Who will make this clear to us? Moses himself. As he tells it, even after some men had observed the Passover outside Jerusalem,

> those men said to him: "We are unclean through touching the dead body of a man; why are we kept from offering the Lord's offering at its appointed time among the people of Israel?" And Moses said to them, "Wait, that I may hear what the Lord will command concerning you." The Lord said to Moses, "Say to the people of Israel, If any man of you or of your descendants is unclean through touching a dead body, or is afar off on a journey, he shall still keep the passover to the Lord. In the second month on the fourteenth day in the evening, they shall keep it".[10]

(7) He means something such as this. If anyone be away from home in the first month. let him not keep the Passover outside the city; but let him return to Jerusalem and keep it in the second month. Let him disregard the time so as not to fail in the matter of the city. In this way, he shows that observance of the place is more necessary than observance of the time.

(8) But what could the Jews say if they observe the Passover outside the city of Jerusalem? Since they transgress in the more necessary matter of place, their observance in the less-important matter of time cannot be urged in their defense. The result is that they are guilty of the worst transgression of the Law, even if it is obvious a thousand times over that they are not neglecting the matter of time.

(9) This is certain not only from what I have said but also from the prophets. What excuse would the Jews of today have when it is clear that the Jews of old never offered sacrifice, nor sang hymns in an alien land, nor did they observe any such fasts as they do today? To be sure, the Jews of old were expecting to recover the way of life in which they could observe these rituals. Therefore, they remained obedient to the Law and did what it commanded, for the Law told them to expect this. But the Jews of today have no hope of recovering their forefathers' way of life. In what prophet can they find proof that they will? They have no hope,

---

[10] Num. 9:8-11

but they cannot bear to give up these practices. And yet, even if they were expecting to recover the old way of life, even so, they ought to be imitating those holy men of old by neither fasting nor observing any other such ritual.

V

(1) To prove to you that the Jews in exile observed none of these rituals, hear what they said to those who asked them to do so. For their barbarian captors were urging them by force and demand to play their musical instruments. "Sing us one of the songs of Zion!"[11] they said. But the Jews clearly understood that the Law commanded them not to do so. Therefore, they said: "How shall we sing the Lord's song in a foreign land?"[12] And, again, the three boys who were captives in Babylon said; "And at this time there is no prince, or prophet, or leader, no burnt offering, or sacrifice, or oblation, or incense, no place to make an offering before thee or to find mercy".[13] Certainly there was much room for a place of sacrifice in the country, but since the temple was not there, they steadfastly refrained from offering sacrifice.

(2) And again God spoke to his people through the lips of Zechariah: "When you fasted and mourned in the fifth month and in the seventh, for these 70 years, was it for me that you fasted?"[14] He was speaking of the captivity. Tell me: By what right, then, do you Jews fast today, when your ancestors neither offered sacrifices, nor fasted, nor kept the feasts? And this makes it especially clear that they did not observe the Passover. Where there was no sacrifice, there no festival was held, because all the feasts had to be celebrated with a sacrifice.

(3) Let me provide proof for this very point. Listen to the words of Daniel: "In those days, I, Daniel, was mourning for three weeks. I ate no delicacies, no meat or wine entered my mouth, nor did I anoint myself at all, for the full three weeks. On the 24th day of the first month, as I was standing on the bank of the great river, that is, the Tigris, I lifted up my eyes and looked, and behold, a man clothed in linen, whose loins were

---

[11] Ps. 137:3
[12] Ps. 137:4
[13] Song of Three Young Men 1:15
[14] Zech. 7:5

girded with gold of Uphaz".[15] Pay careful heed to me here, for this text makes it clear that they did not observe the Passover. Let me tell you how this is. The Jews were not permitted to fast during the days of the feast of unleavened bread. But for 21 days, Daniel took no food at all. And what proves that the 21 days included the days of the feast of unleavened bread? We learn this from what he said, namely, that it was on the 24th day of the first month.

(4) But the Passover comes to an end on the 21st of that month. If they began the feast on the 14th day of the first month and then continued it for seven days, they then come to the 21st. Nonetheless, Daniel steadfastly continued his fast even after the Passover had come and gone. For if Daniel had begun his fast on the third day of the first month and then continued through a full 21 days, he passed the 14th, went on for seven days after that, and then kept fasting for three more days.

(5) How, then, do the Jews of today avoid being cursed and defiled? The holy ones of old followed no such observances of what the Law prescribed, because they were in a strange land. Are today's Jews doing just the opposite, so that they may stir up contentiousness and strife? If some of the holy ones of old who spoke and acted this way were lax and irreverent, perhaps we would have considered their failure to observe these precepts as a sign of their laxity. But they loved and revered God, they gave their very lives for what God had decreed. So it is abundantly clear that failure to keep the Law was not the result of their laxity. Rather, their failure to keep the Law was prompted by the Law itself, because the Law said they must not observe those rituals outside Jerusalem.

(6) This brings us to a conclusion on another matter of great importance: the observances regarding sacrifices, Sabbaths, new moons, and all such things prescribed by the Jewish way of life of that day were not essential. Even when they were observed, they could make no great contribution to virtue; when neglected, they could not make the excellent man worthless, nor degrade in any way the sanctity of his soul. But those men of old, while still on Earth, manifested by their piety a way of life that rivals the way the angels live. Yet they followed none of these observances, they slew no beasts in sacrifice, they kept no feast, they made no display of fasting. But they were so pleasing to God that they surpassed

---

[15] Dan. 10:2-5

this human nature of ours and, by the lives they lived, they drew the whole world to a knowledge of God.

(7) Who could match a Daniel? Who could match the three boys in Babylon? Did they not anticipate the greatest commandment which the Gospels give, the commandment which is the chief source of all blessings? Had they not already proved this by their deeds? For John says: "Greater love has no man than this, that a man lay down his life for his friends".[16] But they laid down their lives for God.

(8) We must admire them for this. But we must also admire them because they were not doing it for any reward. This is why the boys in Babylon said: "Our God whom we serve is able to deliver us from the burning fiery furnace; and he will deliver us out of your hand, O king. But if not, be it known to you, O king, that we will not serve your gods".[17] The prophet means: The reward is sufficient for us that we are dying for God. And they gave proof of this great virtue even though they were observing none of the Law's prescriptions.

VI

(1) You Jews will say: "Why, then, did God impose these prescriptions if he did not wish them observed?" And I say to you: If he wished them observed, why, then, did he destroy your city? God had to do one or the other of two things if he wished these prescriptions to remain in force: either he had to command you not to sacrifice in one place, since he intended to scatter you to every corner of the world; or, if he wished you to offer sacrifice only in Jerusalem, he was obliged not to scatter you to every corner of the world and he should have made that one city impregnable, because it was there alone that sacrifice has to be offered.

(2) Again the Jews will say: "What is this, then? Was God contradicting himself when he ordered the Jews to sacrifice in one place but then barred them from that very place?" By no means! God is very consistent. He did not wish you to offer sacrifices from the beginning, and I bring forward as my witness of this the very prophet who said: "Hear the word of the Lord, you rulers of Sodom! Give ear to the teaching of our God, you people of Gomorrah!"[18] But it was really to the Jews the

---

[16] John 15:13
[17] Dan. 3:17-18
[18] Isa. 1:10

prophet spoke, not to those dwelling in Sodom and Gomorrah. Yet he calls the Jews by the names of these people because, by imitating their evil lives, the Jews had developed a kinship with those who dwelt in those cities.

(3) In fact, Isaiah called the Jews 'dogs' and Jeremiah called them 'mare-mad horses.' This was not because they suddenly changed natures with those beasts but because they were pursuing the lustful habits of those animals. "What to me is the multitude of your sacrifices?"[19] says the Lord. But it is clear that those who dwelt in Sodom never offered sacrifices. Isaiah is aiming his remarks against the Jews when he calls them by the name of those brute animals, and he does so for the reason I just mentioned. "What care I for the number of your sacrifices?" says the Lord; "I have had enough of burnt offerings of rams and the fat of fed beasts; I do not delight in the blood of bulls, or of lambs, or of he-goats. When you come to appear before me, who requires of you this trampling of my courts?"[20] Did you hear his voice clearly saying that he did not require these sacrifices from you from the beginning? If he had made sacrifice a necessity, he would also have subjected the first Jews to this way of life and all the patriarchs who flourished before the Jews of Isaiah's day.

(4) Then the Jews will ask: "How is it that he straightway did permit the Jews to sacrifice?" He was giving in to their weakness. Suppose a physician sees a man who is suffering from fever and finds him in a distressed and impatient mood. Suppose the sick man has his heart set on a drink of cold water and threatens, should he not get it, to find a noose and hang himself, or to hurl himself over a cliff. The physician grants his patient the lesser evil, because he wishes to prevent the greater and to lead the sick man away from a violent death.

(5) This is what God did. He saw the Jews choking with their mad yearning for sacrifices. He saw that they were ready to go over to idols if they were deprived of sacrifices. I should say, he saw that they were not only ready to go over, but that they had already done so. So he let them have their sacrifices; the time when the permission was granted should make it clear that this is the reason. After they kept the festival in honor of the evil demons, God yielded and permitted sacrifices. What he all but

[19] Isa. 1:11
[20] Isa. 1:11-12

said was this: "You are all eager and avid for sacrifices. If sacrifice you must, then sacrifice to me." But even if he permitted sacrifices, this permission was not to last forever; in the wisdom of his ways, he took the sacrifices away from them again.

(6) Let me use the example of the physician again—there is really no reason why I should not. After he has given into the patient's craving, he gets a drinking cup from his home and gives instructions to the sick man to satisfy his thirst from this cup and no other. When he has gotten his patient to agree, he leaves secret orders with the servants to smash the cup to bits; in this way, he proposes, without arousing the patient's suspicion, to lead him secretly away from the craving on which he has set his heart.

(7) This is what God did, too. He let the Jews offer sacrifice but permitted this to be done in Jerusalem and nowhere else in the world. After they had offered sacrifices for a short time, God destroyed the city. Why? The physician saw to it that the cup was broken. By seeing to it that their city was destroyed, God led the Jews away from the practice of sacrifice, though it was against their will. If God were to have come right out and said: "Keep away from sacrifice," they would not have found it easy to keep away from this madness for offering victims. But now, by imposing the necessity of offering sacrifice in Jerusalem, he led them away from this mad practice; and they never noticed what he had done

(8) Let me make the analogy clear. The physician is God, the cup is the city of Jerusalem, the patient is the implacable Jewish people, the drink of cold water is the permission and authority to offer sacrifices. The physician has the cup destroyed and, in this way, keeps the sick man from what he demands at an ill-suited time. God destroyed the city itself, made it inaccessible to all, and in this way led the Jews away from sacrifices. If he did not intend to make ready an end to sacrifice, why did God, who is omnipresent and fills the universe, confine so sacred a ritual to a single place? Why did he confine worship to sacrifices, the sacrifices to a place, the place to a time, and the time to a single city, and then destroy the city? It is indeed a strange and surprising thing. The whole world is left open to the Jews, but they are not permitted to sacrifice there; Jerusalem alone is inaccessible to them, and that is the only place where they are permitted to offer sacrifice.

(9) Even if a man be completely lacking in understanding, should it not be clear and obvious to him why Jerusalem was destroyed? Suppose

a builder lays the foundation for a house, then raises up the walls, arches over the roof, and binds together the vault of the roof with a single keystone to support it. If the builder removes the keystone, he destroys the bond which holds the entire structure together. This is what God did. He made Jerusalem what we might call 'the keystone' which held together the structure of worship. When he overthrew the city, he destroyed the rest of the entire structure of that way of life.

VII

(1) Let then my battle with the Jews wait awhile. I did fight a skirmish of words with them today, but I said only what was enough to save our brothers from danger. Perhaps I said much more than that. But I must now exhort those of you who are here in church to show great concern for the fellow members of our body. I do not want to hear you say: "What concern is this of mine? Why interfere and meddle in other people's affairs?"

(2) Our Master died for us. Will you not take the trouble to say a single word? What excuse or defense will you find for this? Tell me this: If you look the other way when so many souls are perishing, how will you find the confidence to stand before the judgment seat of Christ? I wish I could know which ones are running off to the synagogue. Then I would not have needed your help but I would have straightened them out with all speed.

(3) Whenever your brother needs correction, even if you must lay down your life, do not refuse him. Follow the example of your Master. If you have a servant or if you have a wife, be very careful to keep them at home. If you refuse to let them go to the theater, you must refuse all the more to let them go to the synagogue. To go to the synagogue is a greater crime than going to the theater. What goes on in the theater is, to be sure, sinful; what goes on in the synagogue is godlessness. When I say this, I do not mean that you let them go to the theater, for the theater is wicked; I say it so that you will be all the more careful to keep them away from the synagogue.

(4) What is it that you are rushing to see in the synagogue of the Jews who fight against God? Tell me, is it to hear the trumpeters? You should stay at home to weep and groan for them, because they are fighting against God's command, and it is the devil who leads them in

their revels and dance. As I said before, if there once was a time when God did permit what is against his will, now it is a violation of his law and grounds for punishments beyond number. Long ago, when the Jews did have sacrifices, they did sound their trumpets; now God does not permit them to do this.

(5) At least listen to the reason why they got the trumpets. God said to Moses: "Make two silver trumpets; of hammered work you shall make them".[21] Next God explained how the trumpets were to be used, for he went on to say: "You shall blow the trumpets over your burnt offerings and over the sacrifices of your peace offerings".[22]

(6) But where is the altar? Where is the ark? Where is the tabernacle and the holy of holies? Where is file priest? Where are the cherubim of glory? Where is the golden altar of incense? Where is the mercy-seat? Where is the bowl? Where are the drink offerings? Where is the fire sent down from heaven? Did you lose all those and keep only the trumpets? Do you Christians not see that what the Jews are doing is mockery rather than worship?

(7) I blame the Jews for violating the Law. But I blame you much more for going along with the lawbreakers—not only those of you who run to the synagogues but also those of you who have the power to stop the Judaizers but are unwilling to do so. Do not say to me: "What do I have in common with him? He is a stranger, and I do not know him." I say to you that as long as he is a believer, as long as he shares with you in the same mysteries, as long as he comes to the same church, he is more closely related to you than your own kinsmen and friends. Remember, it is not only those who commit robbery who pay the penalty for their crime; those, too, who could have stopped them but did not, pay the same penalty. Those guilty of impiety are punished, and so, too, are those who could have led them from godless ways but did not, because they were too timid or lazy to be willing to do so.

(8) To be sure, the man who buried his money gave it back to his master whole and entire; yet he was punished because he did not make a profit from it. Suppose, then, that you yourself remain pure and free from blame; if you fail to make a profit from your talent, if you fail to bring

---

[21] Num. 10:2
[22] Num. 10:10

back to salvation your brother who is perishing, you will suffer the same punishment which he does.

(9) Is it some great burden I am asking of you, my beloved? Let each one of you bring back for me one of your brothers to salvation. Let each one of you interfere and meddle in your brother's affairs so that we may come to tomorrow's service with great confidence, because we are bringing gifts more valuable than any others, because we are bringing back the souls of those who have wandered away. Even if we must suffer revilement, even if we must be beaten, even if we must endure any other pain whatsoever, let us do everything to win these brothers back. Since these are sick brothers who trample us underfoot, revile us, and rail against us, we are not stung by their insults; we want to see one thing and only one thing: the return to health of him who behaved in this outrageous way.

(10) Many a time a sick man tears the physician's clothes. But the physician does not let this stop him from trying to cure his patient. It is normal, then, for physicians to show such concern for their patients' bodily health. When so many souls are perishing, is it right for us to slacken our efforts and to think we are suffering no terrible harm, even if our own members are rotting with disease? Paul did not think so. What did he say? "Who is weak, and I am not weak? Who is made to fall, and I am not indignant?"[23] See to it that you catch this fire.

(11) Suppose you see your brother perishing. Even if he reviles you, if he insults you, if he strikes you, if he threatens to become your foe, if he menaces you in any other way, show your courage and endure all these insults so that you may win his salvation. If he should become your foe, God will be your friend and will give you in return many great blessings on that day.

(12) May the prayers of the saints save those who have wandered into error, may you who are faithful be successful in your hunt, may those who have blasphemed God be freed from their ungodliness and come to know Christ, who died for them on the cross, so that all of us may, with one accord and one voice, give glory to God and the Father of our Lord Jesus Christ, to whom be glory and power together with the Holy Spirit for ever and ever. Amen.

---

[23] 2 Cor. 11:29

HOMILY V

(1) How is it that we have a larger throng assembled here today? Surely, you have come together to demand that I keep my promise; you are here to receive the silver tried in the fire which I pledged to pay over to you. For as the Psalmist says: "The promises of the Lord are promises that are pure, silver refined in a furnace on the ground".[1] Blessed be God because he has put in your hearts the yearning to hear words good for your souls.

(2) When wine-tipplers get up each morning, they start their meddlesome probing to discover where they will find the day's drinking-bouts, carousals, parties, revels, and drunken brawls; they busy themselves searching for bottles, mixing bowls, and drinking cups. But when *you* get up each day, you go around asking where you will find exhortation and counsel, encouragement, and instruction—the kind of discourse which draws you to give glory to Christ. This makes me the more eager to hold fast to my topic and, from the fullness of my heart, to keep the promises I have made.

(3) My battle against the Jews did come to a fitting end. The monument marking their rout has been set up, the victory crown belongs to me, and I have captured the prize I sought from my previous discourse. For the task I had undertaken was to prove that what the Jews now do, by way of ritual, transgresses and violates the Law. It was my desire to show that in these rites we have men doing battle with God, creatures waging war against him. And with God's help, I did give precise proof of this. For even if the Jews were going to recover their own city, if they were about to return to their old commonwealth and way of life and see their temple rebuilt—an event which will never come to pass—even so, they have no defense for their present practices.

(4) The three boys in Babylon, Daniel, and all the others who spent their days in captivity kept expecting to recover their own city and, after 70 years, to see the soil of their fatherland; they kept looking forward to living again under their ancestral laws. They had a clear pledge and promise that this would come to pass. However, until the promise was

---

[1] Ps. 12:6

fulfilled, until they did return, they did not dare to perform any of the prescribed rites that the Jews do today.

(5) This is the way you, too, can silence and gag the Jews. Ask the Jew why he observes the fast when he has no city. If he shall say: "Because I expect to recover my city," you say to him: "Stop fasting, then, until you do recover it. Certainly, until the holy ones of old returned to their own fatherland, they practiced none of the rites which you now practice. From this it is clear that you are violating the law, even if you are going to recover your city, as you say; you are transgressing your covenant with God and outraging that old commonwealth and way of life." What I have said to your loving assembly both here and in my previous discourse is enough to silence and gag the shameless arguments of the Jews and to prove that they are transgressing the Law.

(6) It was not my sole purpose to stitch shut the mouths of the Jews. I also was anxious to give you more extensive instruction in the teachings of the Church. Come now, and let me give you abundant proof that the temple will not be rebuilt and that the Jews will not return to their former way of life. In this way, you will come to a clearer understanding of what the Apostles taught, and the Jews will be all the more convicted of acting in a godless way. As witness, I shall produce not an angel, not an archangel, but the very Master of the whole world, our Lord Jesus Christ. When he came into Jerusalem and saw the temple, he said: "Jerusalem will be trodden down by the Gentiles, until the times of the Gentiles are fulfilled".[2]

By this he meant the years to come until the consummation of the world. And again, speaking to his disciples about the temple, he made the threat that a stone would not remain upon a stone in that place until the time when it be destroyed. His threat was a prediction that the temple would come to a final devastation and completely disappear.

(7) But the Jew totally rejects this testimony. He refuses to admit what Christ said. What does the Jew say? "The man who said this is my foe. I crucified him, so how am I to accept his testimony?" But this is the marvel of it. You Jews did crucify him. But after he died on the cross, he then destroyed your city; it was then that he dispersed your people; it was

---

[2] Luke 21:24

then that he scattered your nation over the face of the earth. In doing this, he teaches us that he is risen, alive, and in heaven.

(8) Because you were not willing to recognize his power through his benefactions, he taught you by his punishment and vengeance that no one can struggle with or prevail against his might and strength. But even so, you do not believe in him, you do not recognize that he is God and Master of all the world, but you consider him just another man.

(9) Come then and let us conduct a test as we would in the case of a man. How do we test human beings? If we see that a man tells the truth in all things and never ill any way lies to another, we accept his word, even if he happens to be a foe. At least we do so if we have any sense. In the same way, when we see that a man is a liar, even if he tells the truth in some instances, we do not readily accept his word.

II

(1) Let us look, then, at the character and habits of Christ. Not only did he predict and foretell the destruction of the temple but he also prophesied during his life many other things which were going to come to pass a long time afterwards.[3] Let us, then, bring these predictions into the open. If you see that he is lying in these predictions, then do not accept his prediction about the temple, nor consider it deserving of your belief. But if you see that he tells the truth in all things and that this prediction has been fulfilled, if you see that long years have passed but still testify to the truth of what he foretold, let us have no more of your impudence and stubbornness in matters which are clearer than the light of the sun.

(2) Let us see what else he predicted. There once came up to him a woman with an alabaster jar of precious ointment and she poured it on him. His disciples were indignant at what happened and said: "Why was this ointment not sold for 300 denarii and given to the poor?"[4] He reproved them, however, and said "Truly, I say to you, wherever this gospel is preached in the whole world, what she has done will be told in memory of her".[5] Did he or did he not tell the truth? Was his prediction

---

[3] Jesus' prediction is recorded in the Gospel of Mark, which was written around the year 70, shortly after the temple was destroyed by the Romans. Thus, the "prediction" seems to have been written after the actual event.

[4] John 12:5

[5] Matt. 26:13

fulfilled or did it fail to come true? Put these questions to the Jew. Even if he counts his shameless acts in the tens of thousands, he will not be able to look this prophecy in the face and stare it down.

(3) Certainly we do hear her story told in all the churches. Consuls have stood listening to it, and generals, too; men, women, the renowned, the distinguished, the famous ones in every city. Wherever in the world you may go, everyone respectfully listens to the story of her good service; her action is known in every corner of the earth.

(4) How many kings brought many and great blessings on their cities, how many kings waged successful wars, set up many trophies of victory, saved nations, built cities, and in addition, acquired countless revenues? Yet they, for all their great exploits, are buried in the silence of oblivion. Many queens and great ladies have conferred benefits beyond number on those subject to them. Yet some people do not even know them by name. But this worthless woman, who only poured out her ointment, is praised everywhere in the world; the long passage of years has failed to blot out her memory, and the time to come will never quench her fame.

(5) And yet hers was not a deed of renown. For what renown was there in pouring out some ointment? Nor was she a distinguished person, for she was a low woman and an outcast. Nor was there a large audience to see, for only the disciples were gathered around her. Nor was the place one where she could be easily seen. She made no entrance onto a theater stage to perform her service but did her good deed in a house with only ten people present.

(6) Nonetheless, even though she was a lowly person, even though only a few were there to witness it, even though the place was undistinguished, neither these facts nor any others could obscure the memory of that woman. Today, she is more illustrious than any king or queen; no passage of years has buried in oblivion the service she performed.

(7) Tell me, now. How do you explain this? Who brought this about? Is it not the work of the God to whom this service was paid? Is it not God who has spread the story of her deed to every corner of the earth? Is it within the scope of human power to predict such things as these? Who in his right mind could say that? We marvel and are astounded when Christ foretells what he, himself, will do. But when he predicts what others will do and then makes these actions of others clear

to all the world and worthy of every man's belief, it is still more astounding and marvelous.

(8) Again, he said to Peter: "And I tell you, you are Peter, and on this rock, I will build my church, and the powers of death shall not prevail against it".[6] You Jews tell me how you can attack this prediction of his. How can you show that this prophecy is false? The testimony of the facts will not allow it, even if you are obstinate and dispute it ten thousand times. How many conflagrations of war have been kindled against the Church? Many armies have taken the field, many weapons have been used, every form of punishment and torture has been contrived. There were frying-pans, racks, caldrons, ovens, cisterns, cliffs, fangs of wild beasts, seas, confiscations, and ten thousand other means of torture, unmentionable and unendurable. And these were used not only by foreigners but by our own countrymen. Indeed, a sort of civil war held everything in its grip; rather, it was more bitter than any civil war. Not only did citizens do battle with citizens but kinsmen with kinsmen, members of the same household with each other; friends fought friends. Yet none of these things destroyed the Church nor made it weaker.

(9) Certainly, the wonderful and unexpected thing about this is that all these attacks were made against the Church when it was just beginning. If these dread persecutions were let loose against it after it had taken root and after the Gospel message had been planted everywhere in the world, it would not be so strange that the Church had resisted these attacks. But it was at the beginning of her teaching mission, when the seed of faith had just been sown and the understanding of those who heard the word was still somewhat weak, that these violent wars broke out in all their fury. The fact that they did not weaken our position but even made us prosper all the more is the miracle that surpasses all miracles.

(10) You may say that the Church now stands firm because of the peace granted to it by the emperors. To keep you from saying this, God permitted the Church to be attacked and persecuted at a time when it was smaller and seemed to be weaker. God wanted you to learn that the security the Church enjoys today does not come to it from the peace granted by emperors, but front the power of God.

---

[6] Matt. 16:18

III

(1) To help you see the truth of this, consider how many men wished to introduce their teachings among the Greeks and to establish a new commonwealth and way of life. Think of such men as Zeno, Plato, Socrates, Diagoras,[7] Pythagoras, and countless others. Yet they fell so far short of success that many people do not even now know them by name. But Christ not only wrote a constitution but even brought a new way of life to the whole world. How many miracles do they say that Apollonius of Tyana worked? But all his deeds were a fraud, a vain show, and devoid of truth. And you may learn this from the fact that, in an instant, they vanished and disappeared.

(2) Let no one consider it an insult to Christ that, while speaking of him, I mentioned Pythagoras, Plato, Zeno and the man from Tyana. I am not doing this of my own choice but out of consideration for the weakness of the Jews, who see in Christ a mere man. This is what Paul did when he came to Athens. On entering the city, he took the topic for his exhortation not from the prophets or the gospels, but from the Athenians' altar to the unknown God. He did not consider their altar more deserving of faith than the gospels, nor did he account the inscription on it more worthy of honor than the prophets. But he was speaking to pagan Greeks, who believed in none of our sacred books, and so he used arguments from their own beliefs to subdue them. He did the same thing at Corinth when he said: "To the Jews I became as a Jew, in order to win Jews; to those under the law I became as one under the law—though not being myself under the law—that I might win those under the law".[8]

(3) The Old Testament does this, too, in speaking to the Jews about God. It says: "Who is like thee, O Lord, among the gods?"[9] What do you mean, Moses? Is there any comparison at all between the true God and false gods? Moses would reply: "I did not say this to make a comparison; but since I was talking to the Jews, who had a lofty opinion of demons, I condescended to their weakness and brought in the lesson I was teaching in this way." Let me also say that since my discussion is with the Jews,

---

[7] Diagoras of Rhodes (ca. 475 BC) was an Olympic champion boxer also celebrated for his virtuous character.

[8] 1 Cor. 9:20

[9] Exod. 15:11

who consider that Christ is mere man and one who violated their Law, I compared him with those whom the pagan Greeks admire.

(4) If you wish me to make a comparison with men from among the Jews themselves, men who tried to do what Christ did, men who gathered disciples and were proclaimed as leaders and chiefs but who were immediately forgotten, let me try to prove it in this way. Surely this was what Gamaliel did to stop their mouths.[10] When he saw the Sanhedrin in a rage and eager to shed the blood of the disciples, he wished to put a stop to their ungovernable anger. So he gave orders for the apostles to be put outside for a little while and then had this to say to the Jews:

(5) "Men of Israel, take care what you do with these men. For before these days Theudas arose, giving himself out to be somebody, and a number of men, about four hundred, joined him; but he was slain and all who followed him were dispersed and came to nothing. After him Judas the Galilean arose in the days of the census and drew away some of the people after him; he also perished, and all who followed him were scattered. So in the present case I tell you, keep away from these men and let them alone; for if this plan or this undertaking is of men, it will fail; but if it is of God, you will not be able to overthrow them. You might even be found opposing God!"[11]

(6) Where, then, is the proof that if this is the work of men, it will perish? You had proof of this, said Gamaliel, from the cases of Judas and Theudas. So if the man whom the Apostles proclaim is a leader such as Judas and Theudas, if he does not do all he does by the power of God, wait a little while, and the outcome of events will give credibility to what you say. You will know from the way things turn out whether he is a deceiver, as you say, and one who violates the Law, or the God who rules all things and, with ineffable power, orders and arranges our affairs.

(7) And this did come to pass. They did wait. The very outcome of events did prove that his power was divine and unconquerable. That trick which had deceived many men was turned around and back on the devil's own head. When Satan saw that Christ had come, he wished to cover up the reality of his coming and to hide the true purpose of his Incarnation. So he brought on stage the rogues whom we mentioned, so that Christ

---

[10] Acts 5:34
[11] Acts 5:35-39

might be considered one of them. And he did this on the cross, too, when he had two thieves crucified with Christ; he did the same thing in the case of Christ's coming when he strove to conceal the truth by putting it alongside the false. But he failed in both cases, and his very effort provided the strongest proof of Christ's power.

(8) Tell me this. If three men were crucified in the same place, at the same time, by the same judges, why have the two thieves been lost in silence, while He alone is worshipped? Again, if many men introduced new governments, got themselves adherents, and today not even their names are known, how is it that Christ is paid divine service throughout the world?

(9) Comparison makes facts especially clear. You Jews make this comparison, then, and learn how the truth has prevailed. What deceiver has gotten for himself so many churches all over the world, what rogue extended his worship to the ends of the earth, what imposter has every man bowing down before him, and this in the face of ten thousand obstacles? No one did. It is clear, then, that Christ was not a deceiver; he has saved us, he confers blessings upon us, he takes care of us, he protects our lives.

 (10) Let me add one more prediction before I return to the topic on which I proposed to speak. Christ said: "I have not come to bring peace, but a sword".[12] However, he did not speak of what he would himself desire but he was foretelling the end to which things would come. He went on to say: "For I have come to set a man against his father, and a daughter against her mother, and a daughter-in-law against her mother-in-law".[13]

(11) Tell me this. How did he foretell this if he was a mere man and one of the crowd? For this is what he meant. It sometimes happened that in one and the same house one person would believe, and another would not; then the father would want to lead his own son to deny his faith. This is why Christ predicted this very thing. What he was saying was this: "The power of the gospel will be so strong that sons despise their fathers, daughters their mothers, and parents their children. For they will choose

---

[12] Matt. 10:34
[13] Matt. 10:35

not only to scorn members of their own household, but even to lay down their lives, to endure and suffer all things rather than deny their religion."

(12) How could he have managed to know this if he was just another man out of the crowd? How did it occur to him to reach the conclusion that sons would pay greater veneration to him than to their fathers, that parents would find him dearer than their own children, that wives would have a more ardent love for him than for their own husbands? And how did he know that this would happen not in one home only, nor in two, nor three, nor ten, nor twenty, nor a hundred, but in every corner of the world, in every city and country, on land and sea, in populous places and in those with few, if any, dwellings? No one can say that he foretold this and then failed to fulfill his prediction. Certainly it was not only at the very beginning but it is true even today that, because of their religion, many are hated and cast forth from their fathers' houses. However, they pay no heed to this; the fact that they suffer it for the sake of Christ is consolation enough for them.

(13) Tell me this. What human being ever had the power to do this? Yet this man made all these predictions about that woman, about the Church, and about the wars which would be waged against it. He also predicted that the temple would be destroyed, that Jerusalem would be captured, and that the city would no longer be the city of the Jews as it had been in the past.

(14) If he was wrong and deceived you in all those other predictions, and they did not come true, then refuse to believe what he foretold of Jerusalem and the temple. But you do see those other predictions gloriously fulfilled and their truth waxing stronger with each passing day. The gates of hell did not prevail against the Church; after so many years, the story of what that woman did is still told all over the world, and men who believed in him did pay greater veneration to him than to their own parents, wives, and children. If this is true, tell me, why do you reject this one prediction about the temple, especially since the testimony of time puts the gag of silence on your shameless words?

(15) Suppose a mere ten, twenty, thirty, or fifty years were to have passed since the capture of Jerusalem. Even then you would have absolutely no right to show your impudence by rejecting his prediction, but if you wished to be obstinate, you might have had some pretext for protest left to you. But not only fifty years but many more than one, two, or three

centuries have passed since Jerusalem was captured. And never has there been seen a single trace or shadow of the change for which you are waiting. Why, then, are you so rash and foolish as to keep up your shameless objections?

IV

(1) We have said enough to prove that the temple will never be rebuilt.[14] But since the abundance of proofs which support this truth is so great, I shall turn from the gospels to the prophets, because the Jews put their belief in them before all others. And from the words of the prophets I shall make it clear that the Jews will recover neither their city nor their temple in days to come. And yet the need was not mine to prove that the temple will not be restored. This was not my obligation; the Jews have the obligation to prove the opposite, namely, that the temple will be rebuilt. For the years that have elapsed stand by my side in the combat and bear witness to the truth of my words.

(2) Even though the outcome of events defeats them, even though they cannot prove in deeds what they maintain in words, even though they are simply making a rash boast, they have a right to present their testimony. The proof for my position is that the events of which I speak did actually occur; Jerusalem did fall and has not been restored after so many years. Their position rests on their unsupported words.

(3) Yet the burden of proof was on them to show that the city would rise again. This is the procedure for giving proofs in courts of law. Suppose two people are in dispute over some matter, and the first party presents the claim for his position in writing, while the second party attacks his statement. The second party must then bring forward witnesses or other proofs in refutation of what is said in the written deposition; but the plaintiff need not do so. This is what the Jews must now do. They must produce a prophet who says that by all means Jerusalem will be rebuilt. For if there was going to be an end to the present captivity for you Jews, there was every need for the prophets to foretell this, as is clear to anyone who has even so much as glanced at the prophetic books. For it was the custom of old among the Jews that, under inspiration from above, their

---

[14] Indeed, it has yet to be rebuilt, even more than 1,600 years after Chrysostom spoke these words.

prophets would foretell the good or evil things which were going to befall the people.

(4) What was the reason for this? It was because the Jews were so
arrogant and *obstinate*. They immediately forgot what God had done for
them, they ascribed his kindness to demons and reckoned that his blessings had come from them. Even when the sea was divided for them, as
they went forth from Egypt, and while other wonderful things were hap-
pening to them, they forgot the God who was performing these miracles
and attributed them to others who were not gods. For they said to Aaron:
"Up, make us gods who shall go before us".[15] And they said to Jeremiah:
"As for the word which you have spoken to us in the name of the Lord,
we will not listen to you. But we will do everything that we have vowed,
burn incense to the queen of heaven and pour out libations to her, as we
did, both we and our fathers, our kings and our princes, in the cities of
Judah and in the streets of Jerusalem; for then we had plenty of food, and
prospered, and saw no evil. But since we left off burning incense to the
queen of heaven and pouring out libations to her, we have lacked everything and have been consumed by the sword and by famine".[16] The inspired prophets, then, foretold what would happen to the Jews so that
they would ascribe none of the events to idols, but would believe that
both punishments and blessings always come from God; the punishment
came for their sins, and the blessings because of God's love and kindness.

(5) So that you may learn that this is the reason for the prophecy,
hear what Isaiah, the most eloquent of prophets, had to say to the Jewish
people. "Because I know that you are obstinate, and your neck is an iron
sinew" (that is, unbending), "and your forehead brass" (that is, incapable
of blushing). We, too, make a practice of giving the name 'bronze-faced'
to those who cannot blush. And Isaiah went on to say: "The former
things I declared of old, they went forth from my mouth and I made them
known".[17] Then he added the reason for the prophecy when he said:
"Lest you should say, 'My idol did them, my graven image and my mol-
ten image commanded them'".[18]

---

[15] Exod. 32:1
[16] Jer. 44:16-18
[17] Isa. 48:3
[18] Isa. 48:5

(6) At another time some of the Jews who were quarrelsome and boastful and, even after the prophecies were fulfilled, were acting as impudently as if they had never heard them. Then the prophets not only foretold what would come to pass but even had witnesses of what they were doing. Again it was Isaiah who said: "And I got reliable witnesses, Uriah the priest and Zechariah the son of Jeberechiah, to attest for me".[19] And this was not all Isaiah did. He set his prophecy down in writing in a new book so that, after his prophecy was fulfilled, what he had written might bear witness against the Jews of what the inspired prophet predicted to them a long time before. This is why he did not simply write it in a book, but in a new book, a book capable of staying sturdy for a long time without easily falling apart, a book which could last until the events described in it would come to pass.

V

(1) I shall prove that this is true, and that God foretold everything which was going to befall the Jews. I shall do so not only from what Isaiah said but from all the things which happened to them, both good and bad. Indeed, the Jews three times endured bondage, very harsh and most severe; but none of these came upon them unpredicted. God saw to it that each captivity was prophesied. He carefully foretold the place, the duration, the kind, the form of their misfortune, the return from slavery, and everything else.

(2) First, I shall speak of the prediction of their slavery in Egypt. Surely, in speaking to Abraham, God said: "Know of a surety that your descendants will be sojourners in a land that is not theirs, and will be slaves there, and they will be oppressed for four hundred years; but I will bring judgment on the nation which they serve, and afterward they shall come out with great possessions".[20]

Do you see how he mentioned the number of years? Four hundred. The nature of their slavery? He did not simply say: "They shall be subjected to slavery," but: "They will be oppressed." Listen to Moses' explanation of their misfortune. He said: "No straw is given to your servants, yet they say to us, 'Make bricks!'"[21] And each day they were flogged so that

---

[19] Isa. 8:2
[20] Gen. 15:13-14
[21] Exod. 5:16

you may learn the meaning of the words: "[They] will be slaves there, and they will be oppressed." When He said: "I will bring judgment on the nation which they serve," He was speaking of the drowning of the Egyptians in the Red Sea, which Moses described in his canticle when he said: "The horse and his rider he has thrown into the sea".[22] Then he also mentioned the manner of their return when he said that they will return here with great possessions: "That they ask, every man of his neighbor and every woman of her neighbor, jewelry of silver and of gold".[23] Since they had been subjected to slavery a long time and had received no pay, God permitted them to make this demand of the Egyptians even though their masters might be unwilling to pay. And the prophet exclaimed and said: "Then he led forth Israel with silver and gold, and there was none among his tribes who stumbled".[24] So here we have one bondage which was precisely predicted.

(3) Come now and let us turn our discussion to the second captivity. What one is that? The bondage in Babylon. Jeremiah certainly foretold it exactly when he said: "For thus says the Lord: When 70 years are completed for Babylon, I will visit you, and I will fulfil to you my promise and bring you back to this place. For I know the plans I have for you, says the Lord, plans for welfare and not for evil, to give you a future and a hope. Then you will call upon me and come and pray to me, and I will hear you. You will seek me and find me; when you seek me with all your heart, I will be found by you, says the Lord, and I will restore your fortunes and gather you from all the nations and all the places where I have driven you, says the Lord, and I will bring you back to the place from which I sent you into exile".[25] Do you see how here again he spoke of the city, the number of years, and the places from which and to which he was going to lead them?

(4) This explains why Daniel did not make his prayer for the Jews until he saw that the seventy years had elapsed. Who says so? It was Daniel himself, when he said: "And I, Daniel, was overcome and lay sick for some days; then I rose and went about the king's business; but I was

---

[22] Exod. 15:1
[23] Exod. 11:2
[24] Ps. 105:37
[25] Jer. 29:10-14

appalled by the vision and did not understand it".[26] And I understood in the Scriptures the counting of the years of which the Lord spoke to the prophet Jeremiah: that for the ruins of Jerusalem seventy years must be fulfilled. "Then I turned my face to the Lord God, seeking him by prayer and supplications with fasting and sackcloth and ashes".[27]

(5) Did you hear how this bondage was foretold and how the prophet did not dare to bring his prayer and entreaty to God before the appointed time? He feared that his prayer might be rash and in vain. He was afraid he would hear what Jeremiah had heard: "As for you, do not pray for this people, or lift up cry or prayer for them, and do not intercede with me, for I do not hear you".[28] But when he saw that the sentence pronounced against them had been fulfilled and that the time was summoning them to return, he did pray for them. And he did not merely pray, he made his entreaty with fasting, sackcloth, and ashes.

(6) The prophet acted toward God in a way quite common among men. When we see that a master has cast his slaves into prison for many serious crimes, we do not make a plea for them immediately, nor at the outset, nor at the beginning of their punishment. We let them be punished for a few days; then we go to the master with our plea and we have time working on our side. This is exactly what the prophet did. Although the penalty the Jews paid was not as severe as their sins deserved, nonetheless they did pay it. And it was only then that the prophet went to God to plead on their behalf.

(7) If you would like to hear it, let us listen to the prayer he made for them. He said: "I prayed to the Lord my God and made confession, saying, 'O Lord, the great and terrible God, who keeps covenant and steadfast love with those who love him and keep his commandments'".[29] What are you doing, Daniel? When you intercede for those who have sinned and quarreled with God, are you talking about men who keep God's laws? Do those who transgress his commandments deserve pardon? What did Daniel say? "I am not making this prayer for their sake but for the sake of their forefathers, for the sake of Abraham, Isaac, and

---

[26] Dan. 8:27
[27] Dan. 9:3
[28] Jer. 7:16
[29] Dan. 9:4

Jacob".[30] The promise and pledge was made to those who kept God's commandments. These men, then, have no just claim to salvation; this is why I mention their forefathers.

(8) Daniel was not speaking of the Jews in bondage when he said: "Who keeps covenant and steadfast love with those who love him and keep his commandments." That is why he immediately added: "We have sinned and done wrong and acted wickedly and rebelled, turning aside from thy commandments and ordinances; we have not listened to thy servants the prophets".[31] For there is one defense left to sinners after they have sinned: to confess their sins.

(9) Do you now please consider the virtue of the just man and the arrogance of the Jews. He who is conscious of no evil in himself pronounces a most severe judgment on himself when he says: "We have sinned, acted lawlessly, done evil." But those who were fulfilled with ten thousand evils did quite the opposite when they said: "We kept your commandments; and now we call strangers blessed and evildoers are exalted." Just men usually act modestly after they have done just deeds; the wicked generally exalt themselves after they have sinned. The man who was conscious of no wickedness in himself said: "We have acted lawlessly, we have departed from your laws"; those who are aware of the burden of ten thousand sins say: "We have kept your commandments." I tell you this so that we may shun the sinner and emulate the just.

VI

(1) After he ran through their lawless acts, the prophet next spoke of the penalty they paid, because he wanted to use this to win God over to pity them. For he said: "And the curse and oath which are written in the law of Moses the servant of God have been poured out upon us, because we have sinned against him".[32] What is that curse? Do you wish us to read it? "The Lord will bring a nation against you from afar, from the end of the earth, as swift as the eagle flies, a nation whose language you do not understand, a nation of stern countenance, who shall not regard the person of the old or show favor to the young".[33] The three boys in Babylon

---

[30] Chrysostom is paraphrasing here.
[31] Dan. 9:5-6
[32] Dan. 9:11
[33] Deut. 28:49-50

also made this same point clear when they showed that the kind of punishment visited upon them came about because of what they had done. They made confession to God for the sins of all Jews when they said: "You have handed us over to our enemies, lawless and hateful rebels; to an unjust king; the worst in all the world".[34] Do you see how God fulfilled the curse which said: "You will be few in number?" And the one which said: "I shall lead forth against you a shameless nation?

(2) This is the very thing which Daniel was hinting at when he said: "For under the whole heaven there has not been done anything like what has been done against Jerusalem".[35] What evils were these? Mothers ate their own children. Moses foretold this, but Jeremiah shows that it came true. For Moses said: "The most tender and delicately bred woman among you, who would not venture to set the sole of her foot upon the ground because she is so delicate and tender, will grudge to the husband of her bosom, to her son and to her daughter, her afterbirth that comes out from between her feet and her children whom she bears, because she will eat them secretly".[36] But Jeremiah shows that this came true when he said: "The hands of compassionate women have boiled their own children".[37]

(3) But even after he had spoken of the sins of those who had sinned and after he brought into the open the punishment they endured, he did not ask that this should save them. See, then, the prudence of the servant. For after he had made clear that they had not yet paid the penalty their sins deserved, nor had their sufferings discharged the debt for their offenses, he then fled to the mercy of God and the loving-kindness of his way and says: "And now, O Lord our God, who brought your people out of the land of Egypt with a mighty hand, and have made a name for yourself, as at this day, we have sinned, we have done wickedly".[38] What he is saying is: "You did not save the Jews of old for their good actions but because you saw their affliction and distress, because you heard their cry. In the same way, free us from our present evils because of your loving-kindness and because of that alone. We have no other claim to salvation."

---

[34] Dan. 3:32, which is only found in a handful of biblical translations.
[35] Dan. 9:12
[36] Deut. 28:56-57
[37] Lam. 4:10
[38] Dan. 9:15

(4) So he spoke and, after many a lament, he brought forward the city of Jerusalem, like a captive woman, and said: "O Lord, cause thy face to shine upon thy sanctuary, which is desolate. O my God, incline thy ear and hear; open thy eyes and behold our desolations, and the city which is called by thy name".[39] For when he looked among the men and saw no man who could make God propitious, he turned to the buildings and brought up the city. He showed its desolation and, after he completed his discourse on these things, he made God propitious. And this became clear from the events which followed.

(5) But back to what I was talking about. For I must return again to the topic I proposed. Yet I had good reason for bringing in these digressions: I waited to give your minds a brief breathing space, since they were growing weary from the constant conflicts with the Jews. But let me return to the point where I departed from my topic to speak of these matters. Let me prove that the evils which were going to overtake the Jews had been accurately predicted by God's inspiration. My discourse had already shown that those two captivities came upon the Jews neither by chance nor unexpectedly.

(6) It remains for me now to bring up the third captivity. After I have done that, I must speak about the bondage which now encompasses them; I must give clear proof that no prophet ever predicted that there would be any freedom or escape from the ills which now encircle them.

(7) What, then, is this third captivity? It is the bondage that came upon them in the days of Antiochus IV Epiphanes.[40] After Alexander, king of the Macedonians, conquered the Persian king, Darius, he took over the kingdom. After Alexander died, four kings followed him to the throne. Antiochus was the son of one of Alexander's four successors. Many years later, Antiochus burned the temple, laid waste the holy of holies, put an end to the sacrifices, subjected the Jews, and destroyed their whole state.[41]

VII

(1) Daniel foretold all this with the greatest accuracy, even to the very day. He foretold when it would be, how, by whom, the manner of it, where it would find all end, and what change it would bring about. You

---

[39] Dan. 9:17-18
[40] Ruled from 175 to 164 BC.
[41] In 168 BC.

will understand this better after you have heard the vision which the prophet set forth in the form of a parable. The ram is Darius, the Persian king; the goat is the Greek king, Alexander of Macedon; the four horns are Alexander's successors; the last horn is Antiochus himself. But it will be better for you to hear the vision itself.

(2) Daniel said: "And I saw in the vision; and when I saw, I was in Susa the capital, which is in the province of Elam. And I saw in the vision, and I was by the Ulai canal" (The spot in question he calls by a Persian name.) "I raised my eyes and saw, and behold, a ram standing on the bank of the canal. It had two horns, and both horns were high, but one was higher than the other, and the higher one came up last. I saw the ram charging westward and northward and southward; no beast could stand before him, and there was no one who could rescue from his power. He did as he pleased and magnified himself".[42] He was speaking of the Persian power and domain which overran the whole earth.

(3) Next he spoke of Alexander of Macedon and said: "As I was considering, behold, a he-goat came from the west across the face of the whole earth, without touching the ground; and the goat had a conspicuous horn between his eyes".[43] He then spoke of Alexander's encounter with Darius and the victory won by Macedonian might. "He came to the ram with the two horns, which I had seen standing on the bank of the river, and he ran at him in his mighty wrath".—I must cut short the account—"broke his two horns; and the ram had no power to stand before him, but he cast him down to the ground and trampled upon him; and there was no one who could rescue the ram from his power".[44]

(4) After that, Daniel spoke of Alexander's death and the four kings who succeeded him: "But when he was strong, the great horn was broken, and instead of it there came up four conspicuous horns toward the four winds of heaven".[45] Daniel then passed from this point to the reign of Antiochus and showed that he came from one of those four when he said: "Out of one of them came forth a little horn, which grew exceedingly great toward the south, toward the east, and toward the glorious

---

[42] Dan. 8:2-4
[43] Dan. 8:5
[44] Dan. 8:6-7
[45] Dan. 8:8

land".[46] Daniel then went on to show that Antiochus destroyed the Jewish commonwealth and way of life when he said: "And the host was given over to it together with the continual burnt offering through transgression; and truth was cast down to the ground, and the horn acted and prospered".[47] And the holy place will be laid waste and sin replaced the sacrifice. After the altar was destroyed and the holy places trampled underfoot, he set up an idol within and offered unlawful sacrifices to the demons; righteousness was cast to the ground. He both did this and prospered.

(5) Then again, for a second time, he spoke of the same reign of Antiochus Epiphanes, the bondage, and the capture and desolation of the temple; this time, however, he gave the date of these events. He again began, toward the end of the book, with the empire of Alexander and described all the intervening accomplishments of the Seleucids and the Ptolemies in their wars against each other, the exploits of their generals, the strategies, the victories, the armies, the battles fought on land and sea.

When he came to Antiochus, he ended by saying: "Forces from him shall appear and profane the temple and fortress, and shall take away the continual burnt offering" (and by the continuity he meant the uninterrupted daily sacrifices). "And they shall set up the abomination that makes desolate. He shall seduce with flattery those who violate the covenant" (that is, the transgressors among the Jews whom they will remove and keep with themselves); "but the people who know their God shall stand firm and take action" (he means the events in the time of the Maccabees: Judas, Simon, and John). "And those among the people who are wise shall make many understand, though they shall fall by sword and flame" (here again he describes the burning of Jerusalem) "by captivity and plunder, for some days. When they fall, they shall receive a little help" (he means that, in the midst of those evils, they will be able to draw a breath and rise from the dread things which have overtaken them), "And many shall join themselves to them with flattery; and some of those who are wise shall fall".[48] He said this to show that even many of those who stood firm will fall.

(6) Next, Daniel gave the reason why God permitted them to be involved in such trials. What is the reason? "To refine and to cleanse

---

[46] Dan. 8:9
[47] Dan. 10:12
[48] Dan. 11:31-35

them and to make them white, until the time of the end".[49] This is why, said Daniel, God permitted these evils so as to cleanse them and to show who among them was genuine and approved. In telling of the same king's power and might, he said: "He shall do as he pleases, he shall exalt himself and become very powerful." In speaking of the king's blasphemous spirit, he went on to say: "He shall exalt himself and magnify himself above every god, and shall speak astonishing things against the God of gods. He shall prosper till the indignation is accomplished".[50] Daniel was here making it clear that it was not of Antiochus' own will but because of God's wrath against the Jews that he was so victorious.

(7) After Daniel told in many other passages what evils the king would bring on Egypt and Palestine, how he would return, at whose bidding, and under the pressure of what cause, the prophet then recounted a change of fortune and said that, after enduring all these evils, the Jews would find some aid from an angel sent to help them: "At that time shall arise Michael, the great prince who has charge of your people. And there shall be a time of trouble, such as never has been since there was a nation till that time; but at that time your people shall be delivered, every one whose name shall be found written in the book".[51] By that he meant those deserving to be saved.

VIII

(1) But I have not yet given a proof for the question I am investigating. What is that question? That God set a time limit for those involved in these trials, just as he set a limit of 400 years for the exile in Egypt and 70 years for the bondage in Babylon. Let us see, then, if he set any time limit for this third slavery. Where can we find the answer to this? In what Daniel said in the verses following those I discussed.

(2) Since he had heard of the many great evils which would befall the Jews—the burning of Jerusalem, the toppling of their state, the bondage of his people—he then wanted to learn what would be the end of these trials, and if there would be any change in their disastrous condition. So he asked the angel who had appeared to him and said: "O my lord, what shall be the issue of these things? ... Go your way, Daniel," he

---

[49] Dan. 11:35
[50] Dan. 11:36
[51] Dan. 12:1

said, "for the words are shut up and sealed" (indicating the obscurity of the words) "until the time of the end".[52] Then the angel mentioned the reason why God consented to these evils: "Many shall purify themselves, and make themselves white, and be refined; but the wicked shall do wickedly; and none of the wicked shall understand; but those who are wise shall understand".[53]

(3) Next, in predicting the length of time these evils would last, Daniel's angel said: "And from the time that the continual burnt offering is taken away, and the abomination that makes desolate is set up, there shall be 1,290 days".[54] The daily sacrifice was called the continuity, for what is continuous is frequent and unceasing. And among the Jews, it was customary to offer sacrifice to God in the evening and about dawn each day; this is why they called that daily sacrifice a continuity.[55]

(4) But when Antiochus came, he completely did away with this practice. That is what the angel meant when he said: "From the time of the changing of the continuity" (that is, from the time the sacrifice was abolished) "there shall be 1,290 days," that is, three and a half years and a little more. Then to show that there will be an end and deliverance from these woes, the angel went on to say: "Blessed is he who waits and comes to the 1,335 days,"[56] adding 45 days to the 1,290. He did this because it happened that the conflict lasted a month and a half and, in that time, the victory became complete, as did also the deliverance of the Jews from the evils which weighed heavy upon them. And when he said: "Blessed is the man who stands firm 1,335 days," he revealed their deliverance. He did not simply say, "the man who attains," but "the man who stands firm and attains." The reason for this is that many of the unholy ones saw the change, but he does not call them happy; he calls blessed only those who gave witness during the time of troubles, who did not desert their religion, and who then found abatement of their ills. This is why he did not simply say: "the man who attains," but "the man who stands firm and attains."

---

[52] Dan. 12:8-9
[53] Dan. 12:10
[54] Dan. 12:11
[55] The Jews continuously sacrificed live animals, every day, in their temple in Jerusalem. Some reports indicate 40 or 50 animals per day.
[56] Dan. 12:12

(5) What could be clearer than this? Do you see how very carefully the prophet foretold their captivity and release from bondage? He gave the time not in terms of years, or months, but to the very day. That you may know that my words are not based on mere conjecture, come, let us bring in another witness to what I have said, a witness whom the Jews regard with the highest trust, I mean Josephus, who has made their disasters a subject of tragic history and who has paraphrased the entire Old Testament.[57] He was born after Christ's coming and, in speaking of the captivity predicted by Christ, he also discussed this captivity and set forth Daniel's vision about the ram, the goat, the four horns, and the last horn which arose after the others. I do not wish anyone to be suspicious of what I have said; come, then, and let us compare his words with mine.

(6) Josephus praised Daniel and showed exceedingly high admiration for him, setting him above all the other prophets. When he came to the story of Daniel's vision, he had this to say. Daniel left us a book in which he made clear the accuracy and fidelity to truth of his prophecy. For he tells us that after he and some companions had gone forth to a plain at Susa, the metropolis of Persia, suddenly the earth quaked and shook violently. His friends fled and he was left alone. He fell face down and was fixed fast to the spot leaning on both hands. Then someone touched him and at the same time ordered him to get up and see what would happen to his people after many generations

(7) Daniel then arose and was shown a large ram with many horns growing from his head, but the last horn was the highest. Then he looked to the west and saw a goat borne through the air. The goat rushed at the ram, struck him twice with his horns, knocked him to the ground, and trampled on him. Next he saw the goat grown larger and putting forth a very large horn from his forehead. This horn was broken off, but four others grew up, turned to the four winds. As Josephus told the story, Daniel saw a smaller horn rise up from these and it grew strong. God, who showed Daniel the vision, was telling him that war would come upon his nation, that Jerusalem would be taken by storm, the temple would be pillaged, the sacrifices would be hindered and cut short, and that this would last for 1,290 days.

---

[57] Flavius Josephus (37-100 AD) was a Jewish historian who worked for the Romans.

(8) Daniel wrote that he had seen these events in the plain at Susa; he also made it clear that God explained to him what he had seen in the vision. God said that the ram signified the empire of the Persians and Medes, and the horns, those who would hold royal power. He further said that the last horn signified that there would come a king who would surpass those others in wealth and glory. God then explained that the goat would be a ruler from among the Greeks who would twice clash with the Persian king, defeat him in battle, and take over all his empire. The first large horn on the goat's forehead signified the first king. After this fell off, the growth of the four horns and the turning of each of these to the four regions of the earth was a sign that, after the death of the first king, who had neither sons nor family, his successors would divide the empire among them and would rule the world for many years.

(9) And from these successors, the explanation continued, there would arise a king who would make war on the Jewish laws, take away their from of government, pillage their temple, and prevent their sacrifices from being offered for three years. And it did happen that the nation of our fathers underwent these sufferings under Antiochus Epiphanes just as Daniel had seen many years before and had written would come to pass.

IX

(1) What could be clearer than this? Now it is time, unless you think I am making you weary, now it is time to come back to the question we proposed for investigation, namely, the Jews' present slavery and their bondage of today. This was the reason for going through all their exiles. Pay careful heed to me, for our contest is not concerned with ordinary, everyday matters. At the Olympic contests, people have the patience to sit from midnight to noon waiting to see who will win the crown; they take the hot rays of the sun on their bare heads, and do not leave before the winners are decided. Our contest today is not for an Olympic prize but for an incorruptible crown. It would be a shame, then, for us to grow weary and give in to our fatigue.

(2) What I have said has sufficiently proved that the three captivities were predicted, the first lasting for 400 years, the second for 70, and the third for three and a half years. Now let us talk about the present bondage of the Jews. To show that the prophet also predicted this one, I shall offer as my witness that same Josephus, who is on the side of the Jews. Listen

to what he says subsequence to his account of Daniel's vision. He said: "In the same manner, Daniel also wrote about the empire of the Romans and that they would capture Jerusalem and devastate the temple".[58]

(3) Please consider that even if the man who wrote that was a Jew, he did not, on that account, let himself emulate the obstinacy of you Jews. After he said that Jerusalem would be captured, he did not dare to go on to say that it would be rebuilt, nor to mention a definite time for its restoration, because he knew that the prophet had not fixed a definite time. Yet when Josephus spoke previously of the victory of Antiochus and his devastation of Jerusalem, he did state how many days and years the captivity was going to last.

But Josephus said nothing of this sort about the bondage under the Romans. He wrote that Jerusalem and the temple would be despoiled, but he did not add that what had been devastated would be restored. For he saw that the prophet had not added anything about such a restoration. Josephus did say: "All these things, as God revealed them to him, Daniel left behind in his writings, so that those who read them and observe how they have come to pass must wonder that Daniel was so honored by God".[59]

(4) But let us consider where it was that Daniel said that the temple would be despoiled. After he had made his prayer in sackcloth and ashes, Gabriel came to him and said: "Seventy 'sevens' of years [i.e. 490 years] are decreed concerning your people and your holy city";[60] the Jews will say, "he did mention the time." Yes, but the time is not the time of the captivity; what is mentioned is the length of time after which the captivity is going to come upon them. It is one thing to speak of how long the captivity will last and another thing to state the number of years before it will arrive and be upon them.

(5) We read: "Seventy 'sevens' are cut short for your people"; no longer does God say: "for my people." And yet the prophet said: "Let your face shine upon your people," but God thereafter was estranged from them because of the bold crime they were going to commit. Presently the prophet gave the reason: "To finish the transgression, to put an

---

[58] Chrysostom attributes this quote to Josephus' *Antiquities of the Jews*, but the specific citation is unknown.
[59] Ditto, note 58.
[60] Dan. 9:24

end to sin." What does he mean by the words: "To put an end to sin?" What the prophet is saying is that the Jews are committing many sins, but the end of their evil deeds will be the day they slay their Master. Christ also said this: "Fill up, then, the measure of your fathers." "You killed your servants,"[61] he said. "Now add to that the blood of your Master".[62]

(6) See how the thoughts of Christ and Daniel agree, Christ said: "Fill up"; the prophet says: "To finish the transgression, to put an end to sin." What does "end" mean? That no sin thereafter is left to commit. "And until everlasting justice will be introduced." But what is everlasting justice except the justification given by Christ? "To seal both vision and prophet, and to anoint a most holy place".[63] that is, until prophecies shall cease. For this is what is meant by "to seal," namely, to bring anointing to an end, to bring vision to an end. This is why Christ said: "The law and the prophets were until John".[64] Do you see how this threatens utter desolation and the payment for sins and acts of injustice? For God did not threaten that he will forgive the sins of the Jews but that he will execute vengeance upon then.

X

(1) And when did this happen? When were prophecies completely done away with? When was anointing ended so as never again to return? Even if we be silent, the stones will shout out, because the voice of the facts is so clear. For we could not mention a time at which these predictions were accomplished other than the long and many years already past and the years which are going to be longer and more numerous still. Daniel put it more precisely when he said: "And you will know and understand that from the going forth of the word of the answer that Jerusalem was to be rebuilt until the coming of an anointed leader, there will be seven weeks and 62 weeks".[65]

(2) Pay careful attention to me here, because here lies the whole question. The seven weeks and the 62 weeks make 483 years, for he is

---

[61] Matt. 23:32
[62] Matt. 23:35-36
[63] Dan. 9:24
[64] Luke 16:16
[65] Dan. 9:25

here speaking not of weeks of days or months but weeks of years.[66] From Cyrus to Antiochus Epiphanes and the captivity there were 394 years. However, Daniel makes it clear that he is not talking about the destruction of the temple under Antiochus but the subsequent destruction under Pompey, Vespasian, and Titus. He further extends the time and instructs us from what point we must start counting by showing us that our reckoning is not to start from the day of the return from captivity. From what point must we reckon? "Know therefore and understand that from the going forth of the word to restore and build Jerusalem".[67]

(3) Jerusalem, however, was not rebuilt under Cyrus but under Artaxerxes, who was called the Long-handed. For after the return of the Jews, Cambyses was ruler, then the Magians, and after them Darius Hystaspes. Next came Darius' son, Xerxes, and after him Artabanus. After Artabanus, Artaxerxes the Long-handed, ruled Persia. During the twentieth year of his kingship, Nehemiah returned and restored Jerusalem. Ezra has given us an exact account of this. So then, if we count 483 years from this point, we will surely come to the time of the last destruction. And so it is that the prophet said: "It shall be built again with squares and moat".[68] Therefore what he says is this: After the city has been rebuilt and has recovered its own appearance and form, count the 70 weeks from that point and you will see the slavery which has not yet come to an end.

(4) To make still more clear this very point, namely, that the evils which now grip the Jews will not come to an end, he goes on to say: "And after the sixty-two weeks, an anointed one shall be cut off, and shall have nothing; and the people of the prince who is to come shall destroy the city and the sanctuary".[69] Who comes and they will be cut off as in a deluge? There will be no remnant left, nor a root to grow up again, "Its end shall come with a flood, and to the end there shall be war; desolations are decreed".[70]

(5) And again, in speaking of this slavery, he said: "The incense and the offering will be abolished and, furthermore, on the holy place will be the abomination of desolation: and accomplishment shall be given to the

---

[66] Again, for Daniel, a "week" equals 7 years. So 7x7 + 62x7 = 483.
[67] Dan. 9:25
[68] Dan. 9:25
[69] Dan. 9:26
[70] Dan. 9:26

desolation until the end of time." When you hear him say: "Until the end of time," what else is left for you Jews to look forward to? "And furthermore." What does this mean? "Furthermore," that is, in addition to what he has said, that is, in addition to the destruction of the sacrifice and the offering, there will be some other greater evil. What is that evil? "On the holy place will be the abomination of desolation." By the holy place he means the temple; by the abomination of desolation, he means the statue set up in the temple by Antiochus, who destroyed the city.

(6) And he went on to say: "Desolation until the end." It is true that Christ came into the world according to the flesh long after the day of Antiochus Epiphanes, but when he prophesied the captivity to come, he showed that Daniel had predicted it. This was his reason for saying: "So when you see the desolating sacrilege spoken of by the prophet Daniel, standing in the holy place (let the reader understand)".[71] The Jews called every image and statue made by man an abomination. So by his veiled reference to that statue, Daniel showed both when and under whom the captivity would take place. As I showed before, Josephus also assured us that these words were spoken about the Romans.

(7) What is there for me to say to you now that has not already been said? When the prophets predicted the other captivities, they spoke not only of the captivity but also of the length of time it was appointed for each bondage to last; for this present captivity, however, they set no time but, to the contrary, said that the desolation would endure until the end. And to prove that what they said is true, come now and let me offer as witnesses the events themselves.

If the Jews had never attempted to rebuild the temple, they could say: "If we had wished to set our hands to the task and to begin to rebuild it, we could by all means have completed the task." But now I shall show that not once, nor twice, but three times they did attempt it and three times, like wrestlers in the Olympic games, they were thrown to the ground. Therefore, there can be no dispute or question but that the Church has won the victory crown.

---

[71] Matt. 24:15

XI

(1) Yet what kind of men were they who set their hands to the task? They were men who constantly resisted the Holy Spirit, revolutionists bent on stirring up sedition. After the destruction which occurred under Vespasian and Titus, these Jews rebelled during the reign of Hadrian[72] and tried to go back to the old commonwealth and way of life. What they failed to realize was that they were fighting against the decree of God, who had ordered that Jerusalem remain forever in ruins.

(2) But it is impossible for a man to wage war on God and win. So it was that, when these Jews made their attack against the emperor, they forced him again to destroy Jerusalem completely. For Hadrian came and utterly subdued them; he obliterated every remnant of their city. To prevent the Jews from making such an impudent attempt in the future, he set up a statue of himself. But he realized that, with the passage of time, his statue would one day fall. So he gave his own name to the ruined city and, in this way, burned on the Jews a permanent brand which would mark their defeat and testify to the impudence of their revolt. Since he was called Aelius Hadrianus, he ordained that from this name the city was to be called 'Aelia' and to this day it is called by the name of the emperor who conquered it and destroyed it.

(3) Do you see the first attempt of the impudent Jews? Now look at the next. They tried the same thing in the time of Constantine. But the Emperor saw what they tried to do, cut off their ears, and left on their bodies this mark of their disobedience. He then had them led around everywhere, like runaway slaves and scoundrels, so all might see their mutilated bodies and always think twice before ever attempting such a revolt. "Yet these things happened very long ago," the Jews will say. But I tell you that the incident is well known to those of us who are somewhat on in years and are already old men.[73]

(4) But what I am going to tell you is clear and obvious even to the very young. For it did not happen in the time of Hadrian or Constantine, but during our own lifetime, in the reign of the Emperor of 20 years ago. Julian, who surpassed all the emperors in irreligion, invited the Jews to sacrifice to idols in an attempt to drag them to his own level of ungodli-

---

[72] Reigned from 117 to 138 AD.

[73] Chrysostom exaggerates; he was only about 40 years old at the time of delivering these homilies.

ness. He used their old way of sacrifice as an excuse and said: "In the days of your ancestors, God was worshipped in this way."

(5) They refused his invitation, but, at that time, they did admit to the very things I just lately proved to you, namely, that they were not allowed to offer their sacrifices outside Jerusalem. Their answer was that those who offered any sacrifice whatsoever in a foreign land were violating the Law. So they said to the Emperor: "If you wish to see us offer sacrifices, give us back Jerusalem, rebuild the temple, show us the holy of holies, restore the altar, and we will offer sacrifices again just as we did before."

(6) These abominable and shameless men had the impudence to ask these things from an impious pagan and to invite him to rebuild their sanctuary with his polluted hands. They failed to see that they were attempting the impossible. They did not realize that if human hands had put an end to those things, then human hands could get them back for them. But it was God who destroyed their city, and no human power could ever change what God had decreed. "For the Lord of hosts has purposed, and who will annul it? His hand I stretched out, and who will turn it back?"[74] What God has reared up and wishes to remain, no man can tear down. In the same way, what he has destroyed and wishes to stay destroyed, no man can rebuild.

(7) I grant you that the Emperor did give you Jews back your temple and did build you an altar, just as you foolishly suspected he would. But he could not send down to you the heavenly fire from on high, could he? Yet if you could not have this fire, your sacrifice had to be an abomination and unclean. This is why the sons of Aaron perished; they brought in a foreign fire.

(8) Nonetheless, these Jews, who were blind to all things, called on the Emperor for help and begged him to aid them in undertaking to rebuild the temple. The Emperor, for his part, spared no expense, sent engineers from all over the empire to oversee the work, summoned craftsmen from every land; he left nothing undone, nothing untried. He overlooked nothing but worked quietly and a little at a time to bring the Jews to offer sacrifice; in this way, he expected that it would be easy for them to go from sacrifice to the worship of idols. At the same time, in his mad

---

[74] Isa. 14:27

folly, he was hoping to cancel out the sentence passed by Christ which forbade the rebuilding of the temple. But he who catches the wise in their craftiness straightway made clear to him by His action that the decrees of God are mightier than any man's and that works get their strength from the word of God.

(9) They started to work in earnest on that forbidden task, they removed a great mound of earth and began to lay bare the foundations. They were just about to start building when suddenly fire leaped forth from the foundations and completely consumed not only a great number of the workmen but even the stones piled up there to support the structure.[75] This put a stop to the untimely obstinacy of those who had undertaken the project. Many of the Jews, too, who had seen what had happened, were astonished and struck with shame. The Emperor Julian had been madly eager to finish the work. But when he heard what had happened, he was afraid that, if he went on with it, he might call down the fire on his own head. So he and the whole Jewish people withdrew in defeat.

(10) Even today, if you go into Jerusalem, you will see the bare foundation, if you ask why this is so, you will hear no explanation other than the one I gave. We are all witnesses to this, for it happened not long ago but in our own time. Consider how conspicuous our victory is. This did not happen in the times of the good emperors; no one can say that the Christians came and prevented the work from being finished. It happened at a time when our religion was subject to persecution. when all our lives were in danger, when every man was afraid to speak, when paganism flourished. Some of the faithful hid in their homes, others fled the marketplaces and moved to the deserts. That is when these events occurred. So the Jews have no excuse left to them for their impudence.

XII

(1) Are you Jews still disputing the question? Do you not see that you are condemned by the testimony of what Christ and the prophets predicted and which the facts have proved? But why should this surprise me? That is the kind of people you are. From the beginning, you have been shameless and obstinate, ready to fight at all times against obvious facts.

---

[75] A miraculous event, attested to in half a dozen ancient sources.

(2) Do you wish me to bring forward against you other prophets who clearly state the same fact, namely, that your religion will come to an end, that ours will flourish and spread the message of Christ to every corner of the world, that a different kind of sacrifice will be introduced which will put an end to yours? At least listen to Malachi who came later than the other prophets. Let me not at this time bring in the testimony of Isaiah and Jeremiah or the other prophets who came before the captivity. I do not want you Jews to say that their predictions came true during the bondage. Let me bring forward a prophet who came after the return from Babylon and after the restoration of Jerusalem, a prophet who clearly predicted what was to happen to you.

(3) The Jews did return from Babylon, they did recover their city, they did rebuild their temple, and they did offer sacrifices. But it was only after all this that Malachi predicted the coming of the present desolation and the abolition of the Jewish sacrifices. This is what he said, speaking in God's behalf: "I have no pleasure in you, says the Lord of hosts, and I will not accept an offering from your hand. For from the rising of the sun to its setting, my name is great among the nations, and in every place incense is offered to my name, and a pure offering; for my name is great among the nations, says the Lord of hosts. But you profane it when you say that the Lord's table is polluted".[76]

(4) When do you Jews think that this happened? When was incense offered to God in every place? When a pure offering? You could not mention a time other than the time after the coming of Christ. Suppose Malachi did not speak of our time, suppose he did not speak of our sacrifice but of the Jewish sacrifice. Then his prophecy will be opposed to the Law. Moses had forbidden the Jews to bring their sacrifice to any place other than that which the Lord God would choose, and then he confined their sacrifices to one particular place. If Malachi said that sacrifices were going to be offered everywhere and that it would be a pure offering, he was contradicting and opposing what Moses had said.

(5) But there is no contradiction nor quarrel. For Moses spoke about one kind of sacrifice, and Malachi later predicted another. What makes this clear? It is clear both from the prophet's words and also from many other indications. The first indication has to do with the place. For Mala-

---

[76] Mal. 1:10-12

chi predicted that the sacrifice would be offered not in one city, as in the time of the Jewish sacrifice, but "from the rising of the sun even to its setting." The second indication has to do with the kind of sacrifice. By calling it "a pure offering," he showed the kind of sacrifice of which he spoke.

(6) A further indication deals with those who are going to offer this sacrifice. He did not say "in Israel," but "among the nations." He did not want you to think that the worship given in this sacrifice would be confined to one, two, or three cities; therefore, he did not simply say "everywhere," but from the rising of the sun, even to its setting. By these words he showed that every corner of the earth seen by the sun will receive the message of the gospel. He called it a "pure offering," as opposed to the old sacrifice, which was impure. And it was not by its own nature but because of the disposition and intention of those who offered it. This is why the Lord said: "Incense is an abomination to me".[77]

(7) And yet, in other respects, if you should put the two sacrifices side by side to compare them, you will find that the difference between them is so great and unmeasurable that, according to the nature of comparison, only this new sacrifice is properly called pure. Paul contrasted the old Law with the new Law of grace and said that the old Law had been glorified but is now without glory, because of the surpassing glory of the new Law. I, too, would make so bold as to say in this case that, if the new sacrifice should be compared to the old, only this new sacrifice would properly be called pure. For it is not offered by smoke and fat, nor by blood and the price of ransom, but by the grace of the Spirit.

(8) Now hear another prophet who made the same prediction and said that the worship of God would not be confined to one place, but that the time would come when all men would know him. It is Zephaniah who said: "The Lord will be terrible against them; he will shrivel all the gods of the earth, and to him shall bow down, each in its place, all the lands of the nations".[78] Yet this was forbidden to the Jews since Moses commanded them to worship in one place.

(9) You hear that the prophets foretold and predicted that men will no longer be bound to come from all over the earth to offer sacrifice in one city or in one place, but that each one will sit in his own home and

---

[77] Isa. 1:13
[78] Zeph. 2:11

pay service and honor to God. What time other than the present could you mention as fulfilling these prophecies? At any rate, listen to how the gospels and the Apostle Paul agree with Zephaniah. The prophet said: "The Lord shall appear"; Paul said: " For the grace of God has appeared for the salvation of all men," Zephaniah said: "To all nations"; Paul said: "To all men." Zephaniah said: "He will make their gods waste away;" Paul said: "Training us to renounce irreligion and worldly passions, and to live sober, upright, and godly lives in this world".[79]

(10) Again, Christ said to the Samaritan woman: "Woman, believe me, the hour is coming when neither on this mountain nor in Jerusalem will you worship the Father. You worship what you do not know; we worship what we know, *for salvation is from the Jews*. But the hour is coming, and now is, when the true worshipers will worship the Father in spirit and truth, for such the Father seeks to worship him. God is spirit, and those who worship him must worship in spirit and truth".[80] So When Christ said this, he removed from us for the future the obligation to observe one place of worship and introduced a more lofty and spiritual way of worship.

(11) These arguments would suffice to establish that, for the future, there will be no sacrifice, no priesthood, no king among the Jews. Above all, the destruction of the city has proved all these points. But I could also bring forward the prophets as my witnesses, and they distinctly said the same thing. But I see that you have become weary with the length of my discourse; I am afraid that you may think I am foolish and rash to keep annoying you. For this reason, I promise that I will speak to you on this same subject at another time.

(12) Meanwhile, I ask you to rescue your brothers, to set them free from their error, and to bring them back to the truth. There is no benefit in listening to me unless the example of your deeds will match my words. What I said was not for your sakes but for the sake of those who are sick. I want them to learn these facts from you and to free themselves from their wicked association with the Jews. I want them then to show themselves sincere and genuine Christians. I want them to shun the evil

---

[79] Titus 2:12

[80] John 4:21-24. A remarkable passage: Jesus is explicitly stating that "salvation comes from the Jews"—perhaps unsurprising, given that he himself was Jewish.

gatherings of the Jews and their synagogues, both in the city and in the suburbs, because these are robbers' dens and dwellings of demons.

(13) So then, do not neglect the salvation of those brothers. Be meddlesome, be busybodies, but bring the sick ones to Christ. In this way, we shall receive a far greater reward for our good deeds, both in the present life and in the life to come. And we shall receive it by the grace and loving-kindness of our Lord Jesus Christ, through whom and with whom be glory to the Father together with the Holy Spirit, the giver of life, now and forever, world without end. Amen.

Homily VI

(1) Wild beasts are less savage and fierce as long as they live in the forests and have had no experience fighting against men. But when the hunters capture them, they drag them into the cities, lock them in cages, and goad them on to do battle with beast-fighting gladiators. Then the beasts spring upon their prey, taste human flesh and drink human blood. After that, they would find it no easy task to keep away from such a feast but they avidly rush to this bloody banquet.

(2) This has been my experience, too. Once I took up my fight against the Jews and rushed to meet their shameless assaults, I destroyed their reasoning and every lofty thing that exalts itself against the knowledge of God, and I brought their minds into captivity to the obedience of Christ. And after that I somehow acquired a stronger yearning to do battle against them.

(3) But what is the matter with me? You see that my voice has grown weaker and cannot again last for so long a time. I think that what has happened to me is much the same as what happens to a soldier in battle. He cuts to pieces a number of his foes, courageously throws himself against the enemy lines, strews the ground with corpses, but then breaks his sword; disheartened by this mishap, he must retreat to his own ranks. Indeed, what has happened to me is worse. The soldier who has broken his sword can snatch another from some bystander, prove his courage, and show how eager he is for victory. But when the voice becomes weak and exhausted, you cannot borrow another from somebody else.

(4) What shall I do, then? Shall I, too, run away? The power your loving assembly holds over me does not let me run away. I reverence and respect our father, who is here. I reverence and respect your eagerness and earnestness. Therefore, I shall entrust the whole undertaking to his prayers and your charity and I will attempt what lies beyond my power.

(5) It is true that today's feast of the martyrs invites me to recount the conflicts they underwent. If I neglect this topic, if I strip naked and get ready to enter the arena against the Jews, let no one accuse me of choosing the wrong time for my discourse. The martyrs would find a

discourse against the Jews more desirable than any panegyric of mine, since I could never make them more illustrious than they are.

(6) What need could they have of my tongue? Their own struggles surpass our mortal nature. The prizes they won go beyond our powers and understanding. They laughed at the life lived on earth; they trampled underfoot the punishment of the rack; they scorned death and took wing to heaven; they escaped from the storms of temporal things and sailed into a calm harbor; they brought with them no gold or silver or expensive garments; they carried along no treasure which could be plundered, but the riches of patience, courage, and love. Now they belong to Paul's choral band while they still await their crowns, but they find delight in the expectation of their crowns, because they have escaped henceforth the uncertainty of the future.

(7) What need could they have of any words of mine? Therefore, they will find this topic more desirable than any panegyric of mine which, as I said before, will bring no increase to their personal glory. But it could be that they will derive great pleasure from my conflict with the Jews; they might well listen most intently to a discourse given for God's glory. For the martyrs have a special hatred for the Jews since the Jews crucified him for whom they have a special love. The Jews said: "His blood be on us and on our children"; the martyrs poured out their own blood for him whom the Jews had slain. So the martyrs would be glad to hear this discourse.

II

(1) If the present captivity of the Jews were going to come to an end, the prophets would not have remained silent on this but would have foretold it. I gave adequate proof of this when I showed that all their bondages were brought upon them after they had been predicted: the bondage in Egypt, the bondage in Babylon, and the bondage in the time of Antiochus Epiphanes. I proved that for each of these the Sacred Scriptures had proclaimed beforehand both a time and a place. But no prophet defined a duration for the present bondage, although Daniel did predict that it would come, that it would bring total desolation, that it would change their old commonwealth and way of life, and how long after the return from Babylon it would come to pass.

(2) But Daniel did not reveal that it would come to an end nor that these troubles would ever stop. Nor did any other prophet. Daniel did, however, predict the opposite, namely, that this bondage would hold them in slavery until the end of time. The great number of years which have come and gone since that day are witnesses to the truth of what he said. And the years have shown neither trace nor beginning of a change for the better, even though the Jews tried many times to rebuild their temple. Not once, not twice, but three times they tried. They tried in the time of Hadrian, in the time of Constantine, and in the time of Julian. But each time they tried they were stopped. The first two times they were stopped by military force; later it was by the fire which leaped forth from the foundations and restrained them from their untimely obstinacy.

(3) Now I would be glad to ask them a few questions. Why, tell me, did you recover your own country after spending so many years in Egypt? And after you had been again dragged away into Babylon, why did you come back to Jerusalem? Again, in the time of Antiochus, you suffered many evils, but you came back to your old state, you again recovered your sacrifices, your altar, your holy of holies, and all the rest, along with the dignity these things once had. But nothing such as this has happened in your present bondage. One hundred, two hundred, three hundred, four hundred years and many more than that have passed. This is the 500th year up to our own day, but we see no hint of such a change for the better on the horizon. What we do see is that the Jewish fortunes have completely collapsed; they do not even have a dream to show they might have ally expectation such as they had in their former captivities.

(4) Suppose the Jews should plead their sins as an excuse. Suppose they should say: "We sinned against God and offended him. This is the reason why we are not recovering our homeland. We did treat shamelessly the prophets who never ceased to accuse us, we did deny the blood-guilt of which the prophets spoke in tragic phrases, but we will now confess and condemn ourselves for our own sins." If the Jews should plead this excuse, I will be glad to question each one of them again.

(5) Is it because of your sins that you Jews have been living for so long a time outside Jerusalem? What is strange and unusual about that? It is not only now that your people are living sin-filled lives. Did you, in the beginning, live your lives in justice and good deeds? Is it not true that from the beginning and long before today you lived with countless trans-

gressions of the Law? Did not the prophet Ezechiel accuse you ten thousand times when he brought in the two harlots, Oholah and Oholibah, and said "Yet she increased her whoring, remembering the days of her youth, when she played the harlot in the land of Egypt and lusted after her paramours there".[1]

(6) What about this? After the waters of the sea were divided, after the rocks were broken asunder, after so many miracles were worked in the desert, did you not worship the calf? Did you not try many times to kill Moses, now by stoning him, now by driving him into exile, and in ten thousand other ways? Did you ever stop hurling blasphemies at God? Were you not initiated in the rites of Baal of Peor?[2] Did you not sacrifice your sons and daughters to demons? Did you not make a display of every form of ungodliness and sin?

(7) Did not the prophet, speaking in behalf of God, say to you: "For 40 years I loathed that generation and said, 'They are a people who err in heart, and they do not regard my ways'."[3] How was it, then, that at that time God did not turn himself away from you? How is it that after you slew your children, after your idolatries, after your many acts of arrogance, after your unspeakable ingratitude, that God even allowed the great Moses to be a prophet among you and that he worked wondrous and marvelous signs himself? What happened in the case of no human being did happen to you. A cloud was stretched over you in place of a roof; a pillar instead of a lamp served to guide you; your enemies retreated of their own accord; cities were captured almost at the first battle-shout. You had no need of weapons, no need of an army in array, no need to do battle. You had only to sound your trumpets and the walls came tumbling down of their own accord. And you had a strange and marvelous food which the prophet spoke of when he exclaimed: "[He] gave them the grain of heaven. Man ate of the bread of the angels; he sent them food in abundance".[4]

(8) Tell me this. In those days, you were guilty of ungodliness, you worshipped idols, you slew your children, you stoned the prophets, and you did ten thousand dreadful deeds. Why, then, did you enjoy such

---

[1] Ezek. 23:19
[2] A local god of the Moabites.
[3] Ps. 95:10
[4] Ps. 78:24-25

great kindness and good will from Him? Why did He offer you such protection at that time? Now you do not worship idols, you do not slay your children, you do not stone the prophets. Why are you now spending your lives in endless captivity? God was not one kind of God then and a different kind now, was he? Is it not the same God who governed those past events and who brings to pass what goes on today? Tell me this. Why did you have great honor from God when your sins were greater? Now that your sins are less serious, he has turned himself altogether away from you and has given you over to unending disgrace.

(9) If he turns away from you now because of your sins, he should have done so all the more in those days. If he put up with you when you were living lives of ungodliness, he ought to put up with you all the more now that you venture no such enormities. Why, then, has he not put up with you? Even if you are too ashamed to give the reason, I will state it clearly. Rather, I will not state it, but the truth of the facts will do so.

(10) You did slay Christ, you did lift violent hands against the Master, you did spill his precious blood. This is why you have no chance for atonement, excuse, or defense. In the old days, your reckless deeds were aimed against his servants, against Moses, Isaiah, and Jeremiah. Even if there was ungodliness in your acts then, your boldness had not yet dared the crowning crime. But now you have put all the sins of your fathers into the shade. Your mad rage against Christ, the Anointed One, left no way for anyone to surpass your sin. This is why the penalty you now pay is greater than that paid by your fathers. If this is not the reason for your present disgrace, why is it that God put up with you in the old days when you sacrificed your children to idols, but turns himself away from you now when you are not so bold as to commit such a crime? Is it not clear that you dared a deed much worse and much greater than any sacrifice of children or transgression of the Law when you slew Christ?

III

(1) Tell me this. Will you still dare to call Jesus an imposter and lawbreaker? Will you not instead go off and bury yourselves somewhere, when you look the facts in the face, since their truth is so obvious? If Jesus were an imposter and lawbreaker, as you say he was, you should have been held in high honor for putting him to death. Phinehas slew a man and put an end to all God's wrath against the people. The Psalmist

said: "Then Phinehas stood up and interposed, and the plague was stayed".[5] He rescued a great many ungodly men from the wrath of God by slaying a single lawbreaker. This should have happened all the more in your case, if indeed the man you crucified was a transgressor of the Law.

(2) Phinehas, then, was held guiltless after he slew a lawbreaker; indeed, he was honored with the priesthood. But after you crucified an imposter, as you say, who made himself equal to God, you did not receive esteem nor were you held in honor. Instead, you suffered a more grievous punishment than you did when you sacrificed your children to idols. Why is this so? Is it not clear even to the dullest minds? You committed outrage on him who saved and rules the world; now you are enduring this great punishment. Is this not the reason?

(3) Yet even today, you abstain from blood which would defile you and you observe the Sabbath. But at the time you slew Christ, you violated the Sabbath. God even promised, through Jeremiah, to spare your city if you would stop carrying burdens on the Sabbath. Look, you are observing this law now; you are not carrying burdens on the Sabbath. But God is not reconciled to you on this account. Since that sin of yours surpassed all sins, it is useless to say your sins are keeping you from recovering your homeland. You are in the grip of your present sufferings not because of the sins committed in the rest of your lives but because of that one reckless act. If this were not the case, God would not have turned his back on you in such a way, even if you had sinned ten thousand times. This is clear not only from all I have already said but from what I am now going to tell you.

(4) What is this? Oftentimes we have heard God speak to your fathers through the prophets and say: "It is not for your sake, O house of Israel, that I am about to act, but for the sake of my holy name, which you have profaned among the nations to which you came. And I will vindicate the holiness of my great name, which has been profaned among the nations".[6] And again: "It is not for your sake, O house of Israel, that I am about to act, but for the sake of my holy name." What God is saying is this: "You deserved heavier vengeance and punishment. But so that no one may say that God let the Jews stay in the power of their enemies be-

---

[5] Ps. 106:30
[6] Ezek. 36:22-23

cause God was weak and unable to save them, I am helping you and protecting you."

(5) Suppose Christ were a lawbreaker and you crucified him; suppose you had committed countless sins and much worse ones than the sins of your fathers. God would *still* have saved you to keep his name from being profaned. If Christ were a lawbreaker, God would not have let him be considered a great man, God would not want people putting the blame on Christ for your misfortunes. If God clearly overlooks your sins for his glory's sake, he would have done so all the more if you crucified a lawbreaker. He would have approved of this slaughter and would have blotted out your sins, many as they are. But when God clearly and completely turns himself from you, it is obvious that, by his anger and by abandoning you forever, he is proving even to the most shameless that he who was slain was not a lawbreaker, but the lawgiver who has come as the author of countless blessings. You acted outrageously against him and you are now held in indignity and dishonor. We worship him and, even though heretofore we were held in greater dishonor than all of you, now, through the grace of God, we are more venerable than all of you and are held in higher esteem.

(6) But the Jews will say: "Where is the evidence that God has turned away front us?" Does this still need proof in words? Tell me this. Do not the facts themselves shout it out? Do they not send forth a sound clearer than the trumpet's call? Do you still ask for proof in words when you see the destruction of your city, the desolation of your temple, and all the other misfortunes which have come upon you? "But men brought these things upon us, not God." Rather it was God above all others who did these things. If you attribute them to men. then you must consider that, even if men were to have the boldness, they would not have had the power to bring these things to accomplishment, unless it were by God's decree.

(7) The barbarian came down upon you and brought all Persia with him.[7] He expected that he would catch you all by the suddenness of his attack and he kept you all locked up in the city as if you were caught in the net of a hunter or fisherman. Because God was gracious to you at that time—I repeat, at that time without a battle, without a war, without a

---

[7] This occurred when the Assyrian king Sennacherib besieged Jerusalem in 700 BC.

hostile encounter—the barbarian king left 185,000 of his slain soldiers among you and fled, contented that he alone was saved. And God often decided countless other battles in this way. So also now, if God had not deserted you once and for all, your enemies would not have had the power to destroy your city and leave your temple desolate. If God had not abandoned you, the ruin of desolation would not have lasted so long a time, nor would your frequent efforts to rebuild the temple have been in vain.

IV

(1) These are not my only arguments. I shall use other sources as well in my efforts to prevail upon you to agree that it was not by their own power that the Roman emperors did what they did. They did what they did because God was angry with the Jews and had abandoned them. If the things that happened were the work of men, your misfortunes should have ended with the capture of Jerusalem and your disgrace should not have gone beyond it. Let me grant, according to your argument, that men demolished the walls, destroyed the city, and overturned the altar; was it the work of men that you have no more prophets? Men did not take away the grace of the Spirit, did they? Did men destroy the other things you held solemn, such as the voice from the propitiatory, the power which came in the anointing, the declaration made by the priest from the stones?

(2) The Jewish religious way of life did not have all its origins from here below; the greater number and the more solemn things came from heaven above. For example, God permitted the sacrifices. The altar was from here below as were the bundles of wood, the knife, and the priest. But the rite which was going to enter the sanctuary and consume the sacrifices had its source from on high; no man carried the fire into the temple, but a flame came down from above and by this the ministry for the sacrifice was fulfilled.

(3) And, again, if they ever had to know something, a voice came forth from the propitiatory, or mercy-seat, from between the cherubim, and foretold the future. Again, from the stones which were on the breast of the high priest, which they called the declaration, there came a sort of flashing which indicated the future. Furthermore, whenever someone had to be chosen and anointed, the grace of the Spirit would wing its way down and the oil would run on the forehead of the elect. Prophets fulfilled these ministries. And many a time a cloud of smoke obscured the

sanctuary. To keep the Jews from continuing their shameless ways and attributing their desolation to men, God not only permitted the city to fall and the temple to be destroyed but he also removed the things which had their source from heaven above: the fire, the voice, the flashing of the stones, and all other such things.

(4) The Jews will tell you: "Men waged war on us; men plotted against us." When they say this, tell them that men would certainly not have waged war against them unless God had permitted it. Granted that men tore down your walls. Did a man keep the fire from coming down from heaven? Did a man stop the voice which was continually heard from the propitiatory? Did a man stop the declaration from the stones? Did a man put an end to the anointing of your priests? Did a man take away all those other things? Was it not God who withdrew them? Surely, this is clear to everybody. Why, then, did God take them away? Is it not obvious that he hated you and turned his back on you once and for all? The Jews will say: "By no means! The reason why we do not have these is because we do not have our mother-city." But why do you not have your mother-city? Is it not because God has abandoned you?

(5) Let us, rather, stop their shameless mouths with still more proof. To do this, let me prove from the Scriptures themselves that the destruction of the temple was not the reason for destroying the ritual given to the prophets. The real reason was the wrath of God. And he is much more provoked to anger now, because of the Jews' mad rage against Christ, than he was when they worshipped the calf. Surely, when Moses was their prophet, there was neither temple nor altar. Even though they kept committing countless acts of ungodliness, his gift of prophecy did not desert him. To be sure, he was a great and noble man, but, in addition to hint, there were again 70 other men who, at that time, were proclaimed as prophets.

(6) This was true not only in Moses' day but also thereafter, when they had been given a temple and the rest of the ritual. Even after this temple was burned and they all had been led off to Babylon, Ezechiel and Daniel saw no holy of holies, stood beside no altar. But even though they were in the middle of a barbarian land and in the midst of unclean transgressors of the Law, they were filled with the Spirit and foretold the future, predicting events far more numerous and marvelous than those

prophesied by their predecessors. And they saw divine visions insofar as it was possible for them to see.

(7) Tell me this. Why is it that you have no prophets now? Is it not clear that it is because God has turned his back on your religion? Why did he turn his back on you? It is again obvious that he did so because of him whom you crucified and because of your recklessness in committing that outrage. What makes this so obvious? It is obvious from this: when you Jews lived the life of ungodliness before, you got everything; now, after the cross, although you seem to be living a more moderate life, you endure a greater vengeance and have none of your former blessings.

V

(1) The prophets clearly and distinctly put the truth before you so that you could learn the reason for your troubles. Hear how Isaiah predicted not only the blessings that will come to all through Christ but also your senseless arrogance. He said: "And with his stripes we are healed".[8] And by these words, he foretold the salvation which has come to all through the cross. Then, to show the kind of men we are, he went on to say: "All we like sheep have gone astray; we have turned everyone to his own way".[9] In describing the manner of his execution on the cross, he said: "As a sheep led to the slaughter or a lamb before its shearer is dumb, so he opens not his mouth. In his humiliation, justice was denied him".[10]

(2) And where can we see that all these things came true? In Pontius Pilate's unlawful court of law. Although they testified to so many things against him, as Matthew said, Jesus made no answer to them. Pilate, the presiding [Roman] official, said to him: "'Have you no answer to make? What is it that these men testify against you?' But he was silent and made no answer."[11] This is what the heaven-inspired prophet meant when he said: "Like a lamb that is led to the slaughter, and like a sheep that before its shearers is dumb, so he opened not his mouth".[12] Then he showed the lawlessness of the law court when he said: "In his humiliation, justice was denied him." No one at that time cast a truly just vote

---

[8] Isa. 53:5
[9] Isa. 53:6
[10] Acts 8:32-33
[11] Mark 14:60-61
[12] Isa. 53:7

against him, but they accepted the false testimony against him. What was the reason for this? Because he did not wish to proceed against them.

(3) If he wished to do so, he would have stirred up everything and shaken the world to its depths. When he was on the cross, he split the rocks, darkened the earth, turned aside the rays of the sun, and made night out of day over the whole world. If he did this on the cross, he could have done it in the courtroom. Yet he did not wish to do it but, instead, showed us his mildness and moderation. This is why Isaiah said: "In his humiliation, justice was denied him." Then, to show that Jesus was not just anybody, he went on to say: "Who shall declare his generation?" Who is this man of whom Isaiah said: "He was cut off out of the land of the living".[13] This is why Paul also said: "Your life is hid with Christ in God. When Christ who is our life appears, then you also will appear with him in glory".[14]

(4) But let me return to the topic which I proposed to discuss and prove, namely, that the Jews are enduring their present troubles because of Christ. It is time now to bring in my witness, Isaiah, who spoke these words. Where, then, did he say this? After he spoke of the trial, death, and ascension, after he said: "He was cut off out of the land of the living." He went on to say: "And they made his grave with the wicked and with a rich man in his death".[15] He did not simply say "the Jews," but "the wicked." What could be more wicked than those who first received so many good things and then slew the author of those blessings?

(5) If these prophecies have not been fulfilled, if you Jews are not now held in dishonor, if you are not now bereft of everything your fathers had, if your city did not fall, if your temple is not in ruins, if your disaster has not surpassed every tragedy, then you Jews should refuse to believe me. But if the facts shout out and prophecy has been fulfilled, why do you keep up your foolish and unavailing impudence?

(6) Where are the things you held as solemn, where is your high priest, where are his robe, his breast piece, and stones of declaration? Do not talk to me about those patriarchs of yours who are hucksters and merchants and filled with all iniquity. Tell me, what kind of priest is he if the ancient oil for anointing priests no longer exists nor any other ritual

---

[13] Isa. 53:8
[14] Col. 3:3-4
[15] Isa. 53:9

of consecration? What kind of a priest is he if there is neither sacrifice, nor altar, nor worship? Do you wish me to speak of the laws governing the priesthood and how priests were consecrated in olden times? In this way, you would find out that those among you who are today called patriarchs are not priests at all. They act the part of priests and are playing a role as if they were on the stage, but they cannot carry the role because they are so far removed from both the reality and even the pretense of priesthood.

(7) Recall how, in those days, Aaron was made a priest, how many sacrifices Moses offered, how many victims he slew, how he bathed Aaron, anointed the lobe of his ear, his right hand, and right foot. Only then did Moses lead Aaron into the holy of holies; only then did he bid him remain there a set number of days. But it is worth your while to hear his very words. "And you shall anoint Aaron and his sons".[16] And the Lord spoke to Moses, saying "Take Aaron and his sons, and the garments, and the anointing oil, and the bull of the sin offering, and the two rams, and the basket of unleavened bread; and assemble all the congregation at the door of the tent of meeting".[17]

> And Moses said to the congregation, 'This is the thing which the Lord has commanded to be done.' And Moses brought Aaron and his sons, and washed them with water. And he put on him the coat, and girded him with the girdle, and clothed him with the robe, and put the ephod upon him, and girded him with the skillfully woven band of the ephod, binding it to him therewith. And he placed the breastpiece on him, and in the breastpiece he put the Urim and the Thummim.[18] And he set the turban upon his head, and on the turban, in front, he set the golden plate, the holy crown, as the Lord commanded Moses. Then Moses took the anointing oil, and anointed the tabernacle and all that was in it, and consecrated them. And he sprinkled some of it on the altar seven times, and anointed the altar and all its

---

[16] Exod. 30:30
[17] Lev. 8:2-3
[18] Two elements of a rabbinical priest's robe, referring to 'lights' and 'perfection,' respectively.

utensils, and the laver and its base, to consecrate them. And he poured some of the anointing oil on Aaron's head, and anointed him, to consecrate him. And Moses brought Aaron's sons, and clothed them with coats, and girded them with girdles, and bound caps on them, as the Lord commanded Moses. Then he brought the bull of the sin offering; and Aaron and his sons laid their hands upon the head of the bull of the sin offering. And Moses killed it, and took the blood, and with his finger put it on the horns of the altar round about, and purified the altar, and poured out the blood at the base of the altar, and consecrated it, to make atonement for it.[19]

After he burned portions of the calf, some within on the altar, others outside the camp, he brought in a ram and offered it for a holocaust.[20]

(8) And again he brought a second ram, the ordination ram. Aaron and his sons laid their hands on it and Moses immolated it. He took some of its blood and put it on the lobe of Aaron's right ear, the thumb of his right hand, and the big toe of his right foot.

And he did the same thing to Aaron's sons. Then he took some parts of the sacrifice and put them into Aaron's hands and those of his sons and in this way, he made the offering. And again he took the blood and some oil and sprinkled Aaron and his vestments with it, and his sons and their vestments. He consecrated them and ordered them to cook the flesh at the entrance to the tent of meeting and to eat it there. And he

---

[19] Lev. 8:5-15

[20] The word 'holocaust' derives from the ancient Jewish word *olah*, meaning 'that which is completely burned.' It was common practice for ancient Jews to completely burn animals as a sacrifice to their god Yahweh (Jehovah); *olah* occurs nearly 300 times in the Old Testament. As noted earlier, from roughly 1000 BC to the year 70 AD, Jews burned an estimated 45 animals per day—around two per hour, day and night, year-round—in their central temple in Jerusalem.

In 310 BC, Greek philosopher Theophrastus wrote about this Jewish practice, using the Greek word *holokautountes*, deriving from 'complete' (*holos*) 'burning' (*kaustos*). This became our English word 'holocaust,' which came into circulation around the year 1200 AD. It is of course highly ironic that 'holocaust,' which today has become a catchword for ultimate evil, was originally a blessed Jewish word.

said: "You shall not go out from the door of the tent of meeting for seven days, until the days of your ordination are completed, for it will take seven days to ordain you".[21]

(9) Moses said that by all these rites Aaron was ordained, purified, and consecrated, and that they appeased God. But we find none of these today: no sacrifice, no holocaust, no sprinkling of blood, no anointing with oil, no tent of meeting where they must sit for a definite number of days. This makes it obvious that the priest among the Jews today is unordained, unclean, under a curse, and profane; he only provokes God's wrath. If a priest could not be ordained in any other way than by these rites, and these rites no longer exist, then there is no possible way that their priesthood could have continued to exist. You see that I was right when I said they had gotten somewhere far off and had been far removed from both the reality and even the pretense of the priesthood.

VI

(1) We can also learn from other sources how awesome was the dignity of the priesthood. Indeed, there was a day when some wicked and evil men revolted against Aaron, quarreled with him over his position in the community, and tried to drive him from his leadership. Moses, the mildest of men, wanted to persuade them by the facts themselves that he had not brought Aaron to the leadership because he was a brother, relative, or member of his family, but that it was in obedience to God's decree that he had entrusted the priesthood to him. So he ordered each tribe to bring a staff, and Aaron was instructed to do the same.

(2) When each tribe had brought a staff, Moses took all of them and put them inside the meeting tent. Once he had put them there, he gave orders that they await the decision of God which would come to them through those staves. Then all the other staves kept their same appearance, but a single one—Aaron's—blossomed and put forth leaves and fruit. So the Lord of nature used leaves instead of letters to teach them that he had again elected Aaron.[22]

(3) God said in the beginning: "Let the earth put forth vegetation",[23] and he stirred up its power to bear fruit; in Aaron's day, he also took that

---

[21] Lev. 8:33
[22] Num. 17:8
[23] Gen. 1:11

dry and fruitless wood and made it blossom without earth or root. That staff was thereafter a proof and witness both of the wickedness of those men and of God's choice. It uttered no word, but the very sight of it, in tones clearer than any trumpet's call, urged every man never to attempt such things as did Aaron's foes.

(4) Not only in this case but at another time and in another way, God made clear his choice of Aaron. Many men conspired against Aaron in their lust for the leadership for which God selected him. (And leadership is the kind of thing many men fight over and desire.) Moses ordered them to bring their censers, put incense in them, and to wait for a decision from heaven. As they were burning their incense, the earth split apart and gulped down all their supporters, and a flame from heaven consumed those who had taken up their censers.[24]

(5) Moses did not want anyone to forget, with the passage of time, what had happened. Nor did he want men of a later day to remain ignorant of God's wondrous decision. Therefore, he gave orders that those bronze censers be picked up and beaten into plates for the altar. Just as the very sight of the voiceless staff sent forth a voice, so these bronze plates would speak to all men thereafter, to exhort and advise them never to imitate the madness of those men of old, for fear that they might suffer the same judgment.

(6) Do you see how priests were chosen in former days? But everything that goes on among the Jews today is a ridiculous sport, a trading in shame, filled with outrages beyond number. Tell me, then. Do you let yourself be led by these men who stubbornly oppose God's laws in their every word and deed? Do you rush to their synagogues? Are you not afraid that a bolt of lightning may come down from above and consume your head? Even if a man is not a thief himself but is seen in a den of robbers, he pays the same penalty as they. You do know this, do you not? But why talk about robbers and their crimes?

(7) Surely you all know and remember the time when some evil tricksters in our midst tore down the statues? You remember how not only those who did this reckless deed but also those who were seen simply standing there when it happened were all arrested and dragged off to court together. And you remember that they all paid the supreme penalty.

---

[24] Num. 16:31

Tell me, then. Are you all agog to run off to a place where they outrage the Father, blaspheme the Son, and reject the Holy Spirit, the giver of life? Are you not afraid, do you not shudder to set foot inside those profane and unclean places? Tell me. What defense or excuse will you have since it is you who have thrust yourself into ruin and perdition, since it is you who have hurled yourself from the precipice?

(8) Do not tell me that the Law and the books of the prophets are there. These do not make it a holy place. Which is the better thing? Is it better to have the books there or to speak out the truths they contain? Obviously it is better to speak out these truths and to keep them in your heart. Tell me, what about this? The devil quoted Scripture. This did not make his mouth holy, did it? You cannot say it did, since the devil kept on being the devil. What about the demons? Just because they spoke out and proclaimed: "These men are servants of the Most High God, who proclaim to you the way of salvation",[25] do we on this account rank them among the apostles? By no means! Just as before, we keep right on turning our backs on them and hating them.

(9) If spoken words do not make the mouth holy, does the presence of the Scriptures make a place holy? But how could this be right? This is my strongest reason for hating the synagogue: it does have the Law and the prophets. And now I hate it more than if it had none of these. Why is this? Because in the Law and the prophets they have a great allurement and many a snare to attract the more simple-minded sort of men. This is why Paul drove out the demon which did not remain silent but spoke out. As the author of Acts says: "But Paul was annoyed, and turned and said to the spirit, 'I charge you in the name of Jesus Christ to come out of her'."[26] Why? Because the demon kept shouting: "These men are servants of the Most High God."

(10) As long as the demons remained silent, they did not deceive people by their words; when they spoke out, they did so with the intention of enticing many of the simpler sort into listening and heeding them in these other matters. The demons wish to open the door to their deceits and to create confidence in their lies. And so they give some admixture

---

[25] Acts 16:17
[26] Acts 16:18

of truth, in the same way that those who mix lethal drugs smear the lip of the cup with honey to make the harmful potion easy to drink.

(11) This is why Paul was very much grieved and why he hurried to stop up the demons' mouths when they took to themselves a dignity which ill became them. *This is why I hate the Jews.* Although they possess the Law, they put it to outrageous use. For it is by means of the Law that they try to entice and catch the more simpleminded sort of men. If they refused to believe in Christ because they did not believe in the prophets, the charge against them would not be so severe. As it is, they have deprived themselves of every excuse because they say that they do believe in the prophets but they have heaped outrage on him whom the prophets foretold.

VII

(1) In short, if you believe the place is holy because the Law and the books of prophets are there, then it is time for you to believe that idols and the temples of idols are holy. Once, when the Jews were at war, the people of Ashdod conquered them, took their ark, and brought it into their own temple. Did the fact that it contained the ark make their temple a holy place? By no means! It continued to be profane and unclean, as the events straightway proved. For God wanted to teach the enemies of the Jews that the defeat was not due to God's weakness but to the transgressions of those who worshipped him. And so the ark, which had been taken as booty in war, gave proof of its own power in an alien land by twice throwing the idol to the ground so that the idol was broken. The ark was so far from making that temple a holy place that it even openly attacked it.

(2) Look at it in another way. What sort of ark is it that the Jews now have, where we find no propitiatory, no tables of the law, no holy of holies, no veil, no high priest, no incense, no holocaust, no sacrifice, none of the other things that made the ark of old solemn and august? It seems to me that the ark the Jews now have is no better off than those toy arks which you can buy in the market place. In fact, it is much worse. Those little toy arks cannot hurt anybody who comes close to them. But the ark which the Jews now have does great harm each day to those who come near it.

(3) "Brethren, do not be children in your thinking; be babes in evil",[27] and rescue from their untimely anguish those who are frightened by these things. Teach them what should really terrify them and make them afraid. They should not be terrified by that ark but they should be afraid that they will bring destruction to the temple of God. How will they destroy the temple of God? By constantly rushing off to the synagogue, by a conscience which is inclined toward Judaism, and by the untimely observance of the Jewish rites.

(4) "You who would be justified by the law; you have fallen away from grace".[28] This is what you must fear. On that day of judgment, you must be afraid of hearing him who will judge you say: "I never knew you; depart from me".[29] In other words, "You made common cause with those who crucified me. You were obstinate toward me and started up again the festivals to which I had put an end. You ran to the synagogues of the Jews who sinned against me. I destroyed the temple and made rains of that august place together with all the awe-inspiring things it contained. But you frequented shrines that are no better than hucksters' shops or dens of thieves".[30]

(5) The cherubim and the ark were still there, the grace of the Spirit still abounded in the temple when Christ said: "You have made it a den of thieves" and "a house of business." And He said this because of the transgressions and blood-guilt of the Jews. Now, after the grace of the Spirit has abandoned them, after all those august solemnities have been taken away, they are still stubborn with God and carry on their irreligious rites. What worthy name can we find to call their synagogues?

(6) The temple was already a den of thieves when the Jewish commonwealth and way of life still prevailed. Now you give it a name more worthy than it deserves if you call it a brothel, a stronghold of sin, a lodging-place for demons, a fortress of the devil, the destruction of the soul, the precipice and pit of all perdition, or whatever other name you give it.

(7) Do you wish to see the temple? Don't run to the synagogue; be a temple yourself. God destroyed one temple in Jerusalem but he reared up temples beyond number, temples more august than that old one ever was.

---

[27] 1 Cor. 14:20
[28] Gal. 5:4
[29] Matt. 7:23
[30] A paraphrase.

Paul said: "You are the temple of the living God".[31] Make that temple beautiful, drive out every evil thought, so that you may be a precious member of Christ, a temple of the Spirit. And make others be temples such as you are yourselves. When you see the poor, you would not find it easy to pass them by. When ally of you see some Christian running to the synagogue, do not look the other way. Find some argument you can use as a halter to bring him back to the Church. This kind of almsgiving is greater than giving to the poor, and the profit from it is worth more than ten thousand talents.

(8) Why do I speak of being worth more than ten thousand talents? Or worth more than the whole visible world? A human being is worth more than the whole world. Heaven and earth and sea and sun and stars were made for his sake.

(9) Consider well, then, the dignity and worth of the man you save. Do not think lightly of the care you show to him. Even if a man gives away more money than you can count, he does not do as great a thing as the man who saves a soul, leads it from its error, and takes it by the hand along the road to godliness. The man who gives to the poor takes away the poor man's hunger; the man who sets a Judaizing Christian straight, wins a victory over godlessness. The first man gave consolation to the poor; the second put a stop to reckless transgression. The first freed the body from pain, the other snatched a soul from the fires of hell.

(10) I showed you the treasure; do not forsake the profit. You cannot dare put the blame on your poverty or excuse yourself because you are indigent. The only expense is one of phrases; the only cost is one of words. Therefore, let us not shrink back from the task but, with all the zeal and desire we possess, let us go hunting for our brothers. Even though they be unwilling, let us drag them into our own houses, let us sit down with them at table and put a meal before them. Let us do this so that after they have broken their fast before our eyes, after they have given us a full and sufficient guarantee of their conversion and return to better ways, they may help both themselves and us to a share in eternal blessings through the grace and loving-kindness of our Lord Jesus Christ, through whom and with whom be glory to the Father together with the Holy Spirit, now and forever, world without end. Amen.

---

[31] 2 Cor. 6:16

HOMILY VII

(1) Have you had enough of the fight against the Jews? Or do you wish me to take up the same topic today? Even if I have already had much to say on it, I still think you want to hear the same thing again. The man who does not have enough of loving Christ will never have enough of fighting against those who hate Christ. Besides, there is another reason which makes a discourse on this theme necessary. These feasts of theirs are not yet over; some traces still remain.

(2) Their trumpets were a greater outrage than those heard in the theaters; their fasts were more disgraceful than any drunken revel. So, too, the tents which at this moment are pitched among them are no better than the inns where harlots and flute-girls ply their trades. Let no one condemn me for the boldness of my words; it is the height of boldness and outrage not to suspect the Jews of these excesses. Since they stubbornly fight against God and resist the Holy Spirit, how can we avoid the necessity of passing such sentence upon them?

(3) This festival used to be a holy one when it was observed according to the Law and at God's command. But this is no longer true. All its dignity has been destroyed because it is observed against God's will. Those who, above all others, treat the Law and the ancient festivals with the least respect are the very ones who are ready today to observe the Law and festivals more than anyone else. But we are the one who honor the Law above all others, even if we let it rest like a man who has grown old and infirm, even if we do not drag it, gray with age, to the arena, even if we do not force it to enter the contests which are not suited to its years. In my past discourses I gave adequate proof that today is not the day of the Law nor of the old commonwealth and the old way of life.

(4) But come now, let me investigate what remains to be discussed. I did enough to complete my task when I proved from all the prophets that any such observance of ritual outside Jerusalem is transgression of the Law and sacrilege. But they never stop whispering in everybody's ear and bragging that they will get their city back again. Even if this were true, they could not escape the charge of transgressing the Law. But I

gave you abundant evidence to prove that the city will not be restored nor will they get back their old commonwealth and way of life.

(5) Once that has been proved, there is no room for disagreement on any of the other points. For example, neither the form of sacrifice, nor of the holocaust, nor the binding force of the Law, nor any other aspect of their old commonwealth and way of life can stand. To begin with, the Law commanded that, three times each year, every male go up to the temple. But they could not do this once the temple was destroyed. Then, too, the Law commanded that sacrifices be offered by the man afflicted with gonorrhea, the leper, the woman in her menstrual period, the woman who had given birth to a child. But this is impossible since the place no longer exists nor is there an altar to be seen. The Law commanded them to sing sacred hymns but, as I showed before, the place they were living in prevented them; the prophets condemned them and said they were reading the Law and making their confession of praise to God in a foreign land. Since they could not even read the Law outside Jerusalem, how could they observe it outside Jerusalem?

(6) This is why God threatened them and said: "I will not punish your daughters when they play the harlot, nor your brides when they commit adultery".[1] What does this mean? First, I shall read to you the old Law and then I shall try to make his meaning clearer. What, then, does the Law say? "If any man's wife goes astray and acts unfaithfully against him, if a man lies with her carnally, and it is hidden from the eyes of her husband, and she is undetected though she has defiled herself, and there is no witness against her, since she was not caught in the act; and if the spirit of jealousy comes upon him and he is jealous of his wife who has defiled herself, or if the spirit of jealousy comes upon him and he is jealous of his wife, though she has not defiled herself".[2]

(7) This is what the Law means. If a woman commits adultery and her husband suspects it, or if he suspects her when she has not committed adultery, but there is no witness nor conception to prove the suspicion, "Then the man shall bring his wife to the priest, and bring the offering required for her, a tenth of an ephah of barley meal".[3] Why, I ask, must it be barley meal rather than fine flour or the meal of wheat? Since what

---

[1] Hosea 4:14
[2] Num. 5:12-14
[3] Num. 5:15

happened was a source of pain, accusation, and wicked suspicion, the form of the sacrifice imitated a household disaster. This is why the Lord said: "He shall pour no oil upon it and put no frankincense on it".[4] Then (for I must cut the account short):

> The priest shall bring her near, and set her before the Lord; and the priest shall take holy water in an earthen vessel, and take some of the dust that is on the floor of the tabernacle and put it into the water. And the priest shall set the woman before the Lord, and unbind the hair of the woman's head, and place in her hands the cereal offering of remembrance, which is the cereal offering of jealousy. And in his hand the priest shall have the water of bitterness that brings the curse. Then the priest shall make her take an oath, saying, "If no man has lain with you, and if you have not turned aside to uncleanness, while you were under your husband's authority, be free from this water of bitterness that brings the curse. But if you have gone astray, though you are under your husband's authority, and if you have defiled yourself, and some man other than your husband has lain with you, then the Lord make you an execration and an oath among your people".[5]

(8) What is the meaning of "an execration and an oath"? As the saying goes: May what happened to that poor woman not happen to me! "May the Lord cause you to become a curse among your people when he makes your womb miscarry and your abdomen swell. May this water that brings a curse enter your body so that your abdomen swells or your womb miscarries. And the woman shall say, 'Amen, Amen'."[6] And it will come to pass, "If she has defiled herself and has acted unfaithfully against her husband, the water that brings the curse shall enter into her and cause bitter pain, and her body shall swell, and her thigh shall fall away, and the woman shall become an execration among her people. But

---

[4] Num. 5:15
[5] Num. 5:16-21
[6] Num. 5:21-22

if the woman has not defiled herself and is clean, then she shall be free and shall conceive children".[7]

Once the Jews had gone off into bondage, none of these things could be done because there was no temple, no altar, no Meeting Tent, no sacrifice to be offered. Because this was the case, when God threatened them, he said: "I will not punish your daughters when they play the harlot, nor your brides when they commit adultery."

II

(1) Do you see that the Law takes its force from the place? And since the city is gone, there can no longer be a priesthood. There can be no emperor if there are no armies, no crown, no purple robe, none of the other things which weld together an empire. So, too, there can be no priesthood if sacrifice has been destroyed, if offerings are forbidden, if the sanctuary has been trampled into the dust, if everything which constituted it has disappeared. For the priesthood depend on all these things.

(2) As I said before, it was enough for my purpose to prove that neither the sacrifices, nor the holocausts, nor the other purifications, nor any other part of the Jewish commonwealth and way of life would return. It was enough, finally, to prove that the temple will never rise again. Now that it is no more, everything has been taken away; if something ritualistic seems to be going on, it is against the Law and a reckless crime. In the same way, once I have proved that the temple will never be restored to its former state, I have at the same time also proved that the rest of the ritual of worship will not return to its former condition, that there will be no priest, there will be no king. If not even a commoner of Jewish blood was allowed to be a servant to foreigners, it would be all the more forbidden for their king himself to be subject to others.

(3) But since my effort and zeal are here devoted not only to stopping up the mouths of the Jews but also to instructing your loving assembly, come now and let me take another authority and prove this same point. Let me prove that both the sacrifices of the Jews and their priesthood have completely ended that day will never again return to their former status.

---

[7] Num. 5:27-28

(4) Who says this? That great and wonderful prophet, David. He made it clear that the one kind of sacrifice would be abolished and another brought in to take its place when he said: "Thou hast multiplied, O Lord my God, thy wondrous deeds and thy thoughts toward us; none can compare with thee!"[8] See how wise the prophet is. He said: "Thou hast multiplied thy wondrous deeds" and he stood aghast at God's power to work miracles. But he did not go on to tell us about the creation of the things we see of heaven, earth, and ocean, of water and fire; he did not tell us of those strange marvels which happened in Egypt, or of any other miracles like those. What did he say were wondrous works? "Sacrifice and offering thou dost not desire".[9]

(5) What do you mean, David? Is this a strange marvel? No, he said. For this was not the only thing he saw. Inspired by heaven, he saw with prophetic eyes how God would lead the nations to him; he saw how those who were nailed to their gods, who worshipped stones, who were worse off than brute beasts suddenly looked up and recognized the Master of all creation; he saw how these men put aside their foul worship of demons and gave pure and bloodless worship to God. At the same time he saw that the Jews, too, who were even more imperfect than the pagans, would put aside their worship through sacrifices, holocausts, and other material things and be led to our way of life. And he pondered on God's ineffable loving-kindness which surpasses all understanding; he stood aghast at how greatly things had changed, how God had reshaped them, how he had made men from demons into angels, and how he had introduced a commonwealth and way of life worthy of heaven.

(6) All this was to take place after the old sacrifice had been abolished and after God had brought into its place the new sacrifice through the body of Christ. This is why David stood aghast and marveled and said: "Thou hast multiplied, O Lord my God, thy wondrous deeds." To show that he made this whole prophetic prediction in behalf of Christ when he said: "Sacrifice and offering thou dost not desire." David went on to say: "But a body hast thou prepared for me".[10] By this he meant the Lord's body which became the common sacrifice for the whole world, the sacrifice which cleansed our soul, canceled our sin, put down death,

---

[8] Ps. 40:5
[9] Ps. 40:6
[10] Ps. 40:6

opened heaven, gave us many great hopes, and made ready all the other things which Paul knew well and spoke of when he exclaimed: "O the depth of the riches and wisdom and knowledge of God! How unsearchable are his judgments and how inscrutable his ways!"[11]

(7) David, then, foresaw all this when he said: "Thou hast multiplied, O Lord my God, thy wondrous deeds" He went to say, speaking in the person of Christ: "Burnt offering and sin offering thou hast not required,"[12] and then continued: "Then I said, 'Lo, I come'."[13] When was 'then'? When the time was ripe for more perfect instructions. We had to learn the less perfect lessons through his servants, but the loftier lessons which surpass the nature of man we had to learn from the Lawgiver himself.

(8) This is why Paul said: "In many and various ways, God spoke of old to our fathers by the prophets; but in these last days he has spoken to us by a Son, whom he appointed the heir of all things, through whom also he created the world".[14] And again, John said: "For the law was given through Moses; grace and truth came through Jesus Christ".[15] And this is the highest panegyric for the Law, namely that it prepared human nature for the Teacher.

(9) But he did not want you to look on him as a new God or any kind of innovation. Hear what he said: "In the roll of the book it is written of me".[16] What he meant was this: "Long ago the prophets foretold my coming and at the beginning of the Scriptures they opened them a little to give men a glimpse of the knowledge that I am God."

III

(1) And so, at the beginning of creation, when God said: "Let us make man in our image, after our likeness",[17] he was revealing to us in a rather obscure way the divinity of his Son, to whom he was then speaking. Later on the Psalmist showed that this new religious way of life did not contradict the old, but that it was God's will that the old sacrifice be abolished

---

[11] Rom. 11:33
[12] Ps. 40:6
[13] Ps. 40:7
[14] Heb. 1:1-2
[15] John 1:17
[16] Ps. 40:7
[17] Gen. 1:26

and the new sacrifice replace the old. The new was an extension of the right way of worship; it did not oppose or fight with the old. He showed this when he said: "In the roll of the book it is written of me" and added: "I delight to do thy will, O my God; thy law is within my heart".[18] And when he explained what God's will was, he made no mention of sacrifice or holocausts or offerings or toil and sweat, but said: "I have told the glad news of deliverance in the great congregation".[19]

(2) What does he mean when he says: "I have told the glad news of deliverance"? He did not simply say: "I have given," "I have told." What does this mean? That he has justified our race not by right actions, nor by toils, not by barter and exchange, but by grace alone. Paul, too, made this clear when he said: "But now the righteousness of God has been manifested apart from law".[20] But the justice of God comes through faith in Jesus Christ and not through any labor and suffering. And Paul took up again the testimony of this Psalm when he spoke as follows: "For since the law has but a shadow of the good things to come instead of the true form of these realities, it can never, by the same sacrifices which are continually offered year after year, make perfect those who draw near".[21] Therefore in coming into the world, he says: "Sacrifices and offerings thou hast not desired, but a body hast thou prepared for me".[22] By this he meant the entrance into the world of the only-begotten, the dispensation through the flesh. For this is the way he came to us. He did not change place—how could he, since he is everywhere and fills all things—but he was made visible to us through the flesh.

(3) Here we are fighting not only against the Jews but also against the pagans and many heretics. So let me uncover for you the deeper meaning here; let me search out the reason why Paul mentioned this text when he had countless testimonies to show that the Law and the old commonwealth and way of life are no longer productive. He did not cite this simply by chance but he did it with good reason and ineffable wisdom. Everybody would agree that he had on this subject other testimo-

---

[18] Ps. 40:8
[19] Ps. 40:9
[20] Rom. 3:21
[21] Heb. 1:10
[22] Heb. 10:5

nies, both of greater length and more vehement, if he had wished to bring them forward.

(4) For example, Isaiah said: "What to me is the multitude of your sacrifices? says the Lord; I have had enough of burnt offerings of rams and the fat of fed beasts; I do not delight in the blood of bulls, or of lambs, or of goats. When you come to appear before me, who requires of you this trampling of my courts? Bring no more vain offerings; incense is an abomination to me".[23] And again, in another place: "Yet you did not call upon me, O Jacob; but you have been weary of me, O Israel! You have not brought me your sheep for burnt offerings, or honored me with your sacrifices. I have not burdened you with offerings, or wearied you with frankincense. You have not bought me sweet cane with money".[24] And Jeremiah said: "To what purpose does frankincense come to me from Sheba, or sweet cane from a distant land? Your burnt offerings are not acceptable, nor your sacrifices pleasing to me".[25] And again: "Add your burnt offerings to your sacrifices, and eat the flesh".[26] And another prophet said: "Take away from me the noise of your songs; to the melody of your harps I will not listen".[27]

And again, there was another text, where the Jews were saying: "Will the Lord be pleased with thousands of rams, with ten thousands of rivers of oil? Shall I give my first-born for my transgression, the fruit of my body for the sin of my soul?"[28] And the prophet reproved them and said: "He has showed you, O man, what is good; and what does the Lord require of you but to do justice, and to love kindness, and to walk humbly with your God?"[29] David also spoke in the same vein when he said: "I will accept no bull from your house, nor he-goat from your folds".[30]

(5) When Paul had so many testimonies in which God surely rejects those sacrifices, the times of the new moon, the Sabbaths, the festivals, why did he omit all these and mention just that one text? Many of the

---

[23] Isa. 1:11-14
[24] Isa. 43:22-24
[25] Jer. 6:20
[26] Jer. 7:21
[27] Amos 5:23
[28] Mic. 6:7
[29] Mic. 6:8
[30] Ps. 50:9

infidels and many of the Jews themselves who are now doing battle with me maintain that their commonwealth and way of life was not abolished because it was imperfect or its place taken by a greater way of life— I mean ours—but because of the sinfulness of those who offered the sacrifices in those days. And Isaiah certainly did say: "When you spread forth your hands, I will hide my eyes from you; even though you make many prayers, I will not listen." Then, to give the reason for this, he went on to say: "Your hands are full of blood".[31] These words are not an accusation made against the sacrifices; they are an indictment of the sinfulness of those who offered them. God rejected their sacrifices because they offered them with bloodstained hands.

(6) Again, when David said: "I will accept no bull from your house, nor he-goat from your folds," he went on to add: "But to the wicked God says, 'What right have you to recite my statutes, or take my covenant on your lips? For you hate discipline, and you cast my words behind you. If you see a thief, you are a friend of his; and you keep company with adulterers. You give your mouth free rein for evil, and your tongue frames deceit. You sit and speak against your brother; you slander your own mother's son'."[32] This makes it clear that in this instance God did not simply reject sacrifices, but that he rejected them because those who offered them were adulterers and thieves and plotted against their brothers. So these enemies of mine maintain that, since each prophet accuses those who offer the sacrifices, his prophecy is saying that this is the reason why God rejected their sacrifices.

IV

(1) This is what my opponents say to me. But Paul dealt them a knockout blow and said enough to shut their shameless mouths when he cited as his witness the text I have discussed. When Paul wished to prove that God had rejected the old commonwealth and way of life because it was imperfect, and that he had rendered it inoperative, he took as testimony that text in which no accusation is made against those who offered the sacrifices. He used a text which makes it clear that the sacrifice was in itself imperfect. For the prophet David made no accusation against the

[31] Isa. 1:15
[32] Ps. 50:16-20

Jews; he simply said: "Sacrifice and offering thou dost not desire; but thou hast given me an open ear. Burnt offering and sin offering thou hast not required".[33]

(2) In explanation of this text Paul said: "He abolishes the first in order to establish the second".[34] If David had said: "Sacrifice and offering thou dost not desire," and then said no more, their argument would have some place to defend itself. But since he also said: "But a body thou hast prepared for me," and showed that another sacrifice was brought in to replace it, he left no hope for the future that the old sacrifice would return. And in explaining this, Paul said: "And by that will we have been sanctified through the offering of the body of Jesus Christ once for all".[35] And also: "For if the blood of goats and bulls and the sprinkling of defiled persons with the ashes of a heifer sanctify for the purification of the flesh, how much more shall the blood of Christ, who through the eternal Spirit offered himself without blemish to God, purify your conscience from dead works to serve the living God?"[36] This gives us abundant proof, then, that those old rituals have stopped, that a new rite has been brought forward to replace them, and that the old will not hereafter be restored.

(3) What is left to discuss now? For some time, I have been anxious to prove to you that their kind of priesthood has disappeared and will never return. Let me make this expressly clear from the Scriptures themselves. First I must preface this with a few remarks, so that my explanation of the scriptures say may be even more obvious.

(4) On his return from Persia, Abraham begot Isaac; Isaac then begot Jacob; Jacob begot the twelve patriarchs from whom arose the twelve tribes—or, rather, the thirteen, because, in Joseph's place, his two sons, Ephraim and Manasseh, became leaders of tribes. A tribe was named after each of Jacob's sons: for example, the tribe of Ruben, of Simeon, of Levi, of Judah, of Naphthali, of Gad, of Asher, of Benjamin. So also in Joseph's case, his two sons, Manasseh and Ephraim, gave their names to two tribes; one was called the tribe of Ephraim and the other the tribe of Manasseh. Of these thirteen tribes, all but one had fields and large in-

---

[33] Ps. 40:6
[34] Heb. 10:9
[35] Heb. 10:10
[36] Heb. 9:13-14

comes, all but one tilled the fields and devoted themselves to all the other secular pursuits. But the tribe of Levi was honored with the priesthood; it alone was freed from secular work. They did not till the farms, nor do anything else of the sort, but devoted their attention exclusively to the priesthood. From all the people, they received tithes of wine and wheat and barley and everything else; all gave them tithes and this was their income. No one from any other tribe could ever become a priest. From this tribe—I mean the tribe of Levi—came Aaron, and by succession, his descendants received the priesthood; no one from another tribe ever becomes a priest. And so these Levites received tithes from the rest and, in this way, supported themselves.

(5) But in the time of Abraham, before the day of Jacob and Isaac, before the coming of Moses, when the Law had not yet been written, when the priesthood did not clearly fall to the Levites, when there was no Meeting Tent or Temple, before the division of the people into tribes, before Jerusalem existed, before anyone at all had yet taken control of the government among the Jews, there was a man named Melchizedek, a priest of the Most High God. This Melchizedek was at the same time both priest and king; he was to be a type of Christ, and Scripture makes clear mention of this. For Abraham attacked the Persians, rescued his nephew Lot from their hands, seized all the spoils, and was returning from his mighty victory over his foes. After describing those events, the Scripture had this to say about Melchizedek: "And Melchizedek king of Salem brought out bread and wine; he was priest of God Most High. And he blessed him and said, 'Blessed be Abram by God Most High, maker of heaven and earth; and blessed be God Most High, who has delivered your enemies into your hand!' And Abram gave him a tenth of everything".[37]

(6) If, then, any prophet clearly says that after Aaron, after that priesthood, after those sacrifices and oblations, there will rise up another priest, not from Levi's tribe but from another tribe from which no one ever became a priest, a priest not according to the order of Aaron but according to the order of Melchizedek, it is just as clear that the old priesthood has ceased to exist and another, a new priesthood has been brought in to take its place. If the old priesthood were going to remain effective, it would have to be called a priesthood according to the order of Aaron and

---

[37] Gen. 14:18-20

not according to the order of Melchizedek. Did any prophet speak of this new priesthood? Yes, that same prophet who before spoke about the sacrifices and who was speaking of Christ when he said: "The Lord says to my Lord: 'Sit at my right hand'."[38]

<h1 style="text-align:center">V</h1>

(1) To prevent anyone from suspecting that this was said about some ordinary man, it was not Isaiah nor Jeremiah, nor any prophet who was a common man that said it, but King David himself. But a king cannot call any man his Lord; it is God alone whom he can call Lord. If David were a common man, perhaps one of those shameless people would have said that he was talking about a mere human being. But now, since David was a king, he would not have called a man his Lord. If David were talking about some ordinary person, how could he have said that this person sat at the right hand of that ineffable and mighty Majesty? That would have been impossible. But of this person said: 'The Lord says to my Lord: 'Sit at my right hand till I make your enemies your footstool.'"

(2) Then, to keep you from thinking that this person was weak and powerless, David went on to say: "Your people will offer themselves willingly on the day you lead your forces on the holy mountains".[39] And he made it still clearer when he said: "From the womb of the morning like dew your youth will come to you".[40] But no mere man was begotten before the dew. "You are a priest forever after the order of Melchizedek".[41] He did not say: "According to the order of Aaron". So ask the Jews why David brought in another priest, according to the order of Melchizedek, if the old priesthood was not going to be abolish.

(3) At any rate, see how Paul made this clearer when he came to this text. After Paul said of Christ: "As he (David) says also in another place. 'You are a priest forever according to the order of Melchizedek',"[42] the Apostle went on to say: "About this we have much to say which is hard to explain, since you have become dull of hearing".[43] After he reproved

---

[38] Ps. 110:1
[39] Ps. 110:3
[40] Ps. 110:3
[41] Ps. 110:4
[42] Heb. 5:6
[43] Heb. 5:11

his disciples—but I must cut the account short—he went on to tell them who Melchizedek was and to tell the story. "[He] met Abraham returning from the slaughter of the kings and blessed him, and to him Abraham apportioned a tenth part of everything".[44] Then, to give some insight into Melchizedek, the type, he said: "See how great he is! Abraham the patriarch gave him a tithe of the spoils".[45] He did not say this for no purpose but because he wanted to show that our priesthood is much greater than the Jewish priesthood. And the excellence of the realities is shown beforehand in the very types which foreshadow them.

(4) Abraham was the father of Isaac, the grandfather of Jacob, and the ancestor of Levi, for Levi was Jacob's son. The priesthood among the Jews began with Levi. So this man Abraham was the ancestor of the Levites and the Jewish priests. But in the time of Melchizedek, who is the type of our priesthood, Abraham had the rank of a layman. Two things make this clear. First, he gave tithes to Melchizedek, and it is the laymen who give tithes to the priests. Second, he was blessed by Melchizedek, and laymen are blessed by priests.

(5) We again see the excellence of our priesthood when we find Abraham, the patriarch of the Jews, the ancestor of the Levites, receiving a blessing from Melchizedek and giving tithes to him. Surely the Old Testament says that Melchizedek blessed Abraham and exacted a tenth part from him. And Paul brought these very points to the fore and said: "See how great he is." Who is 'he'? Paul told us. Melchizedek, "Abraham the patriarch gave him a tithe of the spoils. And those descendants of Levi who receive the priestly office have a commandment in the law to take tithes from the people, that is, from their brethren, though these also are descended from Abraham".[46]

(6) What Paul means is this. He said that the Levites, who were priests among the Jews, received a commandment, according to the Law, to take tithes from the other Jews. Although they all were descended from Abraham, both the Levites and the rest of the people, nonetheless the Levites took tithes from their brothers. But Melchizedek, who was not of their descent, because he was not a descendant of Abraham, and

---

[44] Heb. 7:1-2
[45] Heb. 7:4
[46] Heb. 7:4-5

who was not of the tribe of Levi but from another nation, exacted a tenth part from Abraham, that is, he took tithes from him.

(7) Not only this, but he did something further. What is that? He again blessed Abraham, even though it was Abraham who had received the promises. What does this show? That Abraham was much inferior to Melchizedek. How can this be? "It is beyond dispute that the inferior is blessed by the superior".[47] So that, unless Abraham, the ancestor of the Levites, were inferior to Melchizedek, Melchizedek would not have blessed him, nor would Abraham have given tithes to Melchizedek. But Paul wished to show that, because of the excellence of Melchizedek, that inferiority might have continued, so he went on to say: "One might even say that Levi himself, who receives tithes, paid tithes through Abraham".[48]

(8) What does he mean by "paid tithes"? Although Levi was not yet born, through his father, he, too, gave tithes to Melchizedek. As Paul said: "For he was still in the loins of his ancestor when Melchizedek met him".[49] This is why Paul was careful to say: "So to speak".[50] He went on to tell why he said this. "Now if perfection had been attainable through the Levitical priesthood (for under it the people received the law), what further need would there have been for another priest to arise after the order of Melchizedek, rather than one named after the order of Aaron?"[51]

(9) What is it that Paul meant? He meant this. If the Jewish religion was perfect, if the Law was not a foreshadowing of future blessing but had been efficacious in every respect, if it was not going to yield to another Law; if the old priesthood was not going to disappear and make way for another priesthood, why did the prophet say: "You are a priest forever after the order of Melchizedek?" He should have said: "after the order of Aaron." This is why Paul said: "Now if perfection had been attainable through the Levitical priesthood (for under it the people received the law), what further need would there have been for another priest to arise after the order of Melchizedek, rather than one named after the order of Aaron?"[52]

---

[47] Heb. 7:7
[48] Heb. 7:9
[49] Heb. 7:10
[50] Heb. 7:9
[51] Heb. 7:11
[52] Heb. 7:11

(10) This surely made it clear that the old priesthood was ended and that another much better and more sublime priesthood has been brought in to replace it. When we admit this, we would also agree that another way of life suited to the new priesthood will be brought in and another Law given, and clearly this is ours. Paul prepared us for this when he said: "For when there is a change in the priesthood, there is necessarily a change in the law as well".[53]

(11) Many of the prescriptions of the Law were devoted to the ministries of the priesthood, and the old priesthood has been abolished. Since another priesthood was brought in to replace the old, it is clear also that a greater Law had to be brought in to replace the old. To make clear who it was of whom these words were spoken, Paul said: "For the one of whom these things are spoken belonged to another tribe, from which no one has ever served at the altar. For it is evident that our Lord was descended from Judah, and in connection with that tribe, Moses said nothing about priests".[54]

(12) Christ clearly is sprung from that tribe, namely the tribe of Judah; Christ surely is a priest according to the order of Melchizedek; Melchizedek is surely much more venerable than Abraham. Then we must also admit from every angle that one priesthood is being brought in to replace another and that it is much more sublime than the old priesthood. If the type was such, if it was more magnificent than the Jewish priesthood, the reality which it foreshadowed is itself still much more magnificent. This is the point which Paul was making when he said: "This becomes even more evident when another priest arises in the likeness of Melchizedek, who has become a priest, not according to a legal requirement concerning bodily descent but by the power of an indestructible life".[55]

(13) What did Paul mean when he said: "Not according to a legal requirement concerning bodily descent but by the power of an indestructible life"? He meant that none of Christ's commandments are carnal commandments. He did not order the sacrifice of sheep and calves; he ordered us to worship God through the virtue of our lives; as our reward for this, he set the prize of a life that cannot end. And again, after he had died as the price of our sins, he came and raised us up; he saved us

---

[53] Heb. 7:12
[54] Heb. 7:13-14
[55] Heb. 7:15-16

by freeing us from a double death: the death from sin and the death of the flesh. Since he came bringing us such gifts, Paul said: "Not according to a legal requirement concerning bodily descent but by the power of an indestructible life."

VI

(1) I have, therefore, now proved what was left to be proved. I have proved that, because the priesthood was changed, it was reasonable and necessary that there also be a change of Law. And again I was able to prove this very point by bringing forward as my witnesses the prophets. They testified that the Law will be changed, that the old commonwealth and way of life will be transformed for the better, and that never again will a king arise for the Jews.

(2) But I must say only as much as my audience can listen to and heed; I must not crowd everything together and say it all at once. Therefore, I will store up the rest for another occasion and, for the present, I will stop my instruction at this point. But let me first exhort you, loving assembly, to keep in mind what I have said and to connect it up with what I said before. And what I asked you before, I shall now ask you again. Rescue your brothers and show great concern for our members who have grown negligent. I do not undertake this great task just to hear myself talk or to enjoy the tumult of your applause; I do it to bring those who have been cut off back to the path of truth.

(3) Let no one say to me: "I have nothing in common with him, I would be lucky to manage well my own affairs." No one can manage his own affairs if he does not love his neighbor and work for his salvation. This is what Paul meant when he said: "Let no one seek his own interest, but those of his neighbor".[56] He knew that your own interests lie in what benefits your neighbor. You are in good health, but your brother is sick. So then, if you are in your right mind, you will be distressed over him who is in distress and you will, in this matter, follow the example of that blessed soul who said: "Who is weak, and I am not weak? Who is made to fall, and I am not indignant?"[57]

---

[56] Phil. 2:4
[57] 2 Cor. 11:29

(4) If we find joy in tossing down a couple of obols and spending a little money on the poor, what great pleasure will we reap if we can save men's souls? What recompense will we enjoy in the life to come? Certainly, in this world, as often as we run into these men, we will derive great pleasure from meeting them, because we recall the good turn we did for them. When we see them in the next world before the dread tribunal of judgment, we will experience a great confidence. When the unjust, the greedy, the plunderers, and those who have inflicted countless evils on their neighbors go before this tribunal and see their victims—and they surely will see them, as Christ says, and as is clear from the story of the rich man and Lazarus—they will not be able to open their mouths nor to say a word in their own defense. They will be overwhelmed with the great shame of their condemnation and will be swept off from the sight of their victims into the rivers of flame.

(5) But when those who taught and instructed their neighbors in this life stand before the tribunal, they will see those whom they saved pleading in their behalf. And they will be filled with great confidence and trust. Paul made this clear when he said: "You can be proud of us as we can be of you." Tell me, when will this be? "On the day of our Lord Jesus Christ".[58]

(6) And, again, Christ gave good counsel when he said: "I tell you, use worldly wealth to gain friends for yourselves, so that when it is gone, you will be welcomed into eternal dwellings".[59] You see that much confidence will come to us from those to whom we have done good in this life. But if there are so many prizes, such great recompense, such ample repayment for the money we spent on others, how will we fail to gain many great blessings when we help a soul? Tabitha clothed widows and aided the poor and came back to life from the dead.[60] If the tears of those to whom she did good brought her departed soul back to her body—and this before the day of resurrection—will not the tears of those whom you rescued and saved do something to help you? The widows who stood around Tabitha's corpse pointed out that she who had died was alive. In the same way, those whom you saved in this life will stand around you

---

[58] 2 Cor. 1:14
[59] Luke 16:9
[60] Acts 9:36-42

on the day of judgment. They will snatch you from the fire of Gehenna and to it that you enjoy His loving-kindness in abundance.

(7) Knowing, then, what we now know, let us not be roused to fervor only for the present hour; fan the fire you now have, go forth, and spread salvation over the city; even if you do not know them, get busy and find those who have this sickness. I shall be all the more eager to speak to you when I have found out from your very deeds that I did not scatter my seed on rocky ground. And you yourselves will be more eager to practice virtue. In money matters, the man who has made a profit of two gold pieces gets a greater enthusiasm to collect and amass a profit of ten or twenty pieces. This happens, too, in the matter of virtue. The man who has succeeded in doing a good deed gets some encouragement and motivation from doing this right action. The result is that he will undertake other good deeds.

(8) Let us, then, rescue our brothers and store up beforehand pardon for our sins. Much more, let us first store up abundant confidence and, before all else, let us see to it that God's name is glorified. To do this, let us take our wives, children, and households and go out after this game and quarry. Let us rescue from the snares of the devil those whom he has made captive to his will. And let us not stop until we have done everything in our power to rescue them, whether they heed or reject our words. But it would be impossible, if they are Christians, for them not to heed us.

(9) Still, I do not want you to have even the excuse that they would not heed you. Let me say this. If you pour out many words and do everything in your power and still see that he refuses to heed you, then bring him to the priests. By the help of God's grace, the priests will surely overcome their quarry. But it will all be your doing, because it was you who took him by the hand and led him to us. Let husbands talk to their wives and wives to their husbands, fathers to their children and friends to friends.

(10) Let the Jews learn how we feel. Let it also become known to those who side with the Jews, even though they pretend to be ranked with us. We have an eager and vigilant concern for our brothers who have deserted over to the Jewish side. When the Jews find this out, it will be they, rather than we, who thrust out those of our number who frequent their synagogue. I should say, there will be no one hereafter who will dare to flee to them, and the body of the Church will be unsullied and pure.

HOMILY VIII

(1) Gone is the fasting of the Jews, or rather, the drunkenness of the Jews. Yes, it is possible to be drunk without wine; it is possible for a sober man to act as if he is drunk and to revel like a prodigal. If a man could not get drunk without wine, the prophet would never have said: "Woe to those who are drunk not from wine;"[1] if a man could not get drunk without wine, Paul would never have said: "And do not get drunk with wine".[2] For he said this as if there were a possibility of getting drunk some other way. And it is possible. A man can be drunk with anger, with unseemly desire, with greed, with vainglory, with ten thousand other passions. For drunkenness is nothing other than a loss of right reason, a derangement, and depriving the soul of its health.

(2) Therefore, I would not be making too strong a statement if I should say that we find a drunkard not only in the man who is a heavy drinker of strong wine but also in the man who nurtures some other passion in his soul. For the man in love with a woman who is not his wife, the man who spends his time with prostitutes, is a drunkard. The heavy drinker cannot walk straight, his speech is rude, his eyes cannot see things as they really are. In the same way, the drunkard who is filled with the strong wine of his undisciplined passion is also unsound of speech; everything he utters is disgraceful, corrupt, crude, and ridiculous; he, too, cannot see things as they really are because he is blind to what he sees. Like a deranged man or one who is out of his wits, he imagines he sees everywhere the woman he yearns to ravish. No matter how many people speak to him at gatherings or banquets, at any time or place, he seems not to hear them; he strains after her and dreams of his sin; he is suspicious of everything and afraid of everything; he is no better off than some trapped animal.

(3) Again, the man in the grip of anger is drunk. In the same way as other drunkards, his face became swollen, his voice grows rough, his eyes are bloodshot, his mind is darkened, his reason is submerged, his

---

[1] Isa. 51:21
[2] Eph. 5:18

tongue trembles, his eyes are out of focus, and he does not hear what is really said. His anger affects his brain worse that strong wine; it stirs up a storm and causes a distress that cannot be calmed.

(4) But if the man in the grip of passion or anger is drunk, this is all more true of the impious man who blasphemes God, who goes against his laws and never is willing to renounce his untimely obstinacy. This man is drunk, mad, and much worse off than insane revelers, even if he does not seem aware of his condition. And this is the characteristic which most marks a drunkard: he has no awareness of his unseemly behavior. This, in fact, is the special danger of madness: those who suffer from it do not know they are sick. So, too, the Jews are drunk but do not know they are drunk.

(5) Indeed, the fasting of the Jews, which is more disgraceful than any drunkenness, is over and gone. But let us not stop thinking ahead for our brothers, let us not consider that our concern for them is now no longer timely. See what soldiers do. Suppose they have met the enemy and routed them. As they return from pursuing the foe, they do not immediately rush back to camp. First they go back to the battlefield to pick up their fallen comrades. They bury the dead but, if they see among the corpses some men who are not mortally wounded but are still breathing, they give them as much first aid as they can; they pick them up, and carry them back to their camp. Then they extract the dart, call the physicians, wash away the blood, apply remedies to the wounds, and by giving them every care, they bring the wounded back to health.

(6) Therefore, we must do the same. By God's grace, we made the prophets our warriors against the Jews and routed them. As we return from pursuing out foes, let us look all around to see if any of our brothers have fallen, if the fast has swept some of them off, if any of them have shared in the festival of the Jews. Let us bury no one; let us, however, pick up every fallen man and give him the treatment he needs. In battles between armies of this world, a soldier cannot bring back life or recover for further service a comrade who has fallen once and for all and died. But in a battle of *this* war of ours, even if a man has been mortally wounded, if we have good will and the help of God's grace, we can take him by the hand and lead him back to life. Unlike a casualty in war, here is not a man's body that dies, but his will and his resolution. And it is possible to restore to life a will that has died; it is possible to persuade a

dead soul to come back to its own proper life and to acknowledge again its Master.

II

(1) We must not grow weary, my brothers, we must not become exhausted, we must not lose heart. Let no one say: "We should have done all we could to put them on their guard before the fast. Now that they have fasted, now that they have sinned, now that their transgression is complete, what use is there in helping them now?"

(2) If anyone knows what it means to look out for his brothers, he also knows that he must look for them and show this concern now more than ever. We must not only put them on their guard before they sin but we must also extend a helping hand after they have fallen. Suppose God had done that from the beginning; suppose he had put us on guard only before we sinned; suppose, after we had sinned, he had given us up and let us lie where we had fallen from one end of our life to the other. Then no one of us would ever have been saved.

(3) But God does not act that way. He loves men, he is kind to them, he desires their salvation above all things. And so he looks out for them even after they have sinned. He said to Adam: "You may freely eat of every tree of the garden; but of the tree of the knowledge of good and evil you shall not eat, for in the day that you eat of it you shall surely die".[3] God put Adam on his guard by giving him every warning he would need: he showed him the ease of fulfilling the Law, the liberality of what it permitted, the harshness of the future punishment, and the speed with which it would come. For God did not say: "After one, two, or three days," but, "in the day that you eat of it you shall surely die."

(4) God looked out for Adam very carefully; he instructed him, exhorted him, and gave him many blessings. But even so, Adam disregarded his commands and fell into sin. Still God did not say: "What good will it do now? What is the use of helping now? He ate the fruit, he fell into sin, he transgressed the law, he believed the devil, he dishonored my commandment, he was wounded, he became subject to death and died, he came under the judgment. What need have I to speak to him now?"

---

[3] Gen. 2:16-17

(5) But God said none of these things. Rather, he came immediately to Adam, spoke to him, and consoled him. Again God gave Adam another remedy—the remedy of toil and sweat. God kept right on doing everything and exerting himself until he raised up fallen nature, rescued it from dead, led it by the hand to heaven, and gave it greater blessings than it had lost. By the things God himself did, he taught the devil that he would reap no profit from his plot. Satan had succeeded in driving men from Paradise but he would soon see them in heaven mingling with the angels.

(6) In the case of Cain, God did the same thing. Before Cain's great sin, God spoke plainly to him, warned him, and said: "You sinned; stop it. His (Abel's) refuge is in you and you will rule over him." See God's wisdom and understanding. He said: "Because I have honored Abel, you are afraid he will take from you the privilege of the first-born; you are afraid he will take the first place, which is due to you." For the first-born necessarily had a more honored position than the second-born. So God said: "Take courage, do not be afraid, feel no anguish over this. His refuge is in you, and you will rule over him." This is what God meant: "Stay in the honored position of the first-born; be a refuge, a shelter, and a protection for your brother. But do not jump to bloodshed; do not come to that impious act of murder." Even so, Cain did not listen, he did not stop, he did commit that murder, he did bathe his hands in blood from his brother's throat.

(7) But then what happened? God did not say: "Let him go now. What further use is there in helping him? He did commit the murder, he did slay his brother. He scorned my advice; he dared to do that mad and unforgivable deed of slaughter. Even though I was looking out for him, instructing him, even though he enjoyed such benefice from me, he drove all these from his mind and paid them no heed. Let him go, then, and be hereafter cast from my sight. He has deserved no consideration from me."

(8) God neither said nor did anything like that. Instead, he came again to him, corrected him, and said: "Where is your brother Abel?" When Cain said he did not know, God still did not desert him but he brought him, in spite of himself, to admit what he had done. After Cain said: "I do not know",[4] God said: "The voice of your brother's blood is

---

[4] Gen. 4:9

crying to me from the ground".[5] What God was telling Cain was that the very deed proclaimed who the murderer was. And what did Cain say? "My punishment is greater than I can bear. Behold, thou hast driven me this day away from the ground; and from thy face I shall be hidden".[6]

(9) What Cain meant was this. "I have committed a sin too great for pardon, defense, or forgiveness; if it is your will to punish my crime, I shall lie exposed to every harm because your helping hand has abandoned me." And what did God do then? He said: "Not so! If anyone slays Cain, vengeance shall be taken on him sevenfold".[7] What God said was this: "Do not fear that. You will live a long life. If any man does kill you, he will be subject to many punishments." For the number seven in the Scriptures means an indefinitely large number. So, then, Cain was stricken with many punishments—with torment and trembling, with grief and discouragement, with paralysis of his body. After he had undergone these penalties, as God put it: "And the Lord put a mark on Cain, lest any who came upon him should kill him".[8]

(10) The punishment of which God spoke seems to be excessively harsh but it does give us a glimpse of his great solicitude. God wanted men of later times to exercise self-control; therefore, he designed the kind of punishment which was capable of setting Cain free from his sin. If God had immediately destroyed him, Cain would have disappeared, his sin would have stayed concealed, and he would have remained unknown to men of later days. But as it is, God let him live a long time with that bodily tremor of his. The sight of Cain's palsied limbs was a lesson for all he met; it served to teach all men and exhort them never to dare do what he had done, so that they might not suffer the same punishment. And Cain himself became a better man again. His trembling, his fear, the mental torment which never left him, his physical paralysis kept him, as it were, shackled. They kept him from leaping again to any other like deed of boldness; they constantly reminded him of his former crime; through them he achieved greater self-control in his soul.

---

[5] Gen. 4:10
[6] Gen. 4:13-14
[7] Gen. 4:15
[8] Gen. 4:15

III

(1) As I was speaking, it occurred to me to bring up a further question. Cain confessed his sin and condemned what he had done; he said his crime was too great to be forgiven and that he deserved no defense. Why, then, could he not wash away his sins? The prophet Isaiah said: "Set forth your case, that you may be proved right".[9] Why, then, was Cain condemned? Because he did not tell his sins as the prophet commanded. Isaiah did not simply say: 'Tell your iniquities.' What did he say? He said: 'Be the first to tell your iniquities.'

(2) The question here is this. It is not simply a matter of telling, but of being the first to tell and not waiting for an accuser to convict you. But Cain did not tell first; he waited for God to accuse him. And then, when God did accuse him, he denied it. After God had once and for all given clear proof of what he had done, Cain then told his sin. But this is no longer a confession.

(3) Therefore, beloved, when you commit sin, do not wait for another man to accuse you but, before you are accused and indicted, do you yourself condemn what you have done. Then, if someone accuses you later on, it is no longer a matter of your doing the right thing in confessing, but of your correcting the accusation which he makes. And so it is that someone else has said: "The just man begins his speech by accusing himself".[10] So it is not a question of accusing but of being the first to accuse yourself and not waiting for others to accuse you.

(4) Peter certainly sinned gravely in denying Christ. But he was quick to remind himself of his sin and, before anyone accused him, he told of his error and wept bitterly. He so effectively washed away his sin of denial that he became the chief of the apostles and the whole world was entrusted to him.

(5) But I must get back to my main topic. What I said has given us sufficient proof that we must not neglect or scorn our brothers who fall into sin. We must put them on their guard before they sin and we must show great concern for them after they have fallen. This is what physicians do. They tell people in good health what can preserve their health and what can ward off every disease. But if people have disregarded their

---

[9] Isa. 43:26
[10] Prov. 18:17

instructions and have fallen sick, physicians do not neglect them but, especially at that time, they look out for the patients so that they may free them from their ailments.

(6) And Paul certainly did this too. Incest is a sin and serious transgression which is not even found among the pagans. But Paul did not scorn the man who had committed incest. Even though this man rebelled and refused to be cured, even though he kicked about and was unmanageable, Paul led him back to health and he did it in such a way as to unite him again to the body of the Church. Paul did not say to himself: "What good would it do? What would be the use? He committed incest, he has sinned; he does not want to give up his licentious ways; he is puffed up and boastful and has made his wound incurable. So let us be done with him and leave him in the lurch."

(7) Paul said none of these things. The very reason why he showed great concern for this sinner was that he saw the man had slipped into unspeakable wickedness. So Paul never gave up frightening him, threatening him, punishing him both through his own efforts and with the help of others. Paul left nothing undone, nothing untried until he brought the man to acknowledge his sin, to see his transgression. And, at last, Paul freed the man from every stain of sin.

(8) Now you do the same thing Paul did. Imitate the Samaritan in the gospel who showed such concern for the man who had been wounded. For a Levite passed that way, a Pharisee passed by, but neither of them turned to the man lying there. They just went their way and, like the cruel, pitiless men they were, they left him there. But a Samaritan, who was in no way related to this man, did not hurry past but stopped, took pity on him, poured oil and wine on his wounds, put him on his own animal, and brought him to an inn. There he gave some money to the innkeeper and promised him more for taking care of a man who was in no way related to him.

(9) He did not say to himself: "What do I care about him? I am a Samaritan. I have nothing in common with him. We are far from the city and he cannot even walk. What about this? Suppose he is not strong enough to make the long journey. Am I going to bring in a corpse, will I be arrested for murder, will I be held accountable for his death?" Many a time people go along a road and see men who have been wounded but are still breathing. But they pass them by not because they are stingy with

their money, but because they are afraid that they themselves may be dragged into court and held accountable for the murder.

(10) That gentle and benevolent Samaritan feared none of these things. He scorned all such fears, put the man on his own beast, and brought him to an inn. He did not think of any of these things—neither the danger, nor the expense, nor anything else. If the Samaritan was so kind and gentle to a stranger, what excuse would we have for neglecting our brothers when they are in deeper trouble? For those who have just observed the fast have fallen among robbers, the Jews. And the Jews are more savage than any highwaymen; they do greater harm to those who have fallen among them. They did not strip off their victim's clothes nor inflict wounds on his body as did those robbers on the road to Jericho. The Jews have mortally hurt their victim's soul, inflicted on it ten thousand wounds, and left it lying in the pit of ungodliness.

IV

(1) Let us not overlook such a tragedy as that. Let us not hurry past so pitiable a sight without taking pity. Even if others do so, you must not. Do not say to yourself: "I am no priest or monk; I have a wife and children. This is a work for the priests; this is work for the monks." The Samaritan did not say: "Where are the priests now? Where are the Pharisees now? Where are the teachers of the Jews?" But the Samaritan is like a man who found some great store of booty and got the profit.

(2) Therefore, when you see someone in need of treatment for some ailment of the body or soul, do not say to yourself: "Why did so-and-so or so-and-so not take care of him?" You free him from his sickness; do not demand an accounting from others for their negligence. Tell me this. If you find a gold coin lying on the ground, do you say to yourself: "Why didn't so-and-so pick it up?" Do you not rush to snatch it up before somebody else does?

(3) Think the same way about your fallen brothers; consider that tending his wounds is like finding a treasure. If you pour the word of instruction on his wounds like oil, if you bind them up with your mildness, and cure them with your patience, your wounded brother has made you a richer man that any treasure could. Jeremiah said: "If you utter

what is precious, and not what is worthless, you shall be as my mouth".[11] What could we compare to that? No fasting, no sleeping on the ground, no watching and praying all night, nor anything else can do as much for you as saving your brother can accomplish.

(4) Consider how frequent and numerous are the sins you commit with your mouth. How many obscene things has it said? How many blasphemies, how many abuses has it uttered? If you give some thoughts to this, you will surely never hesitate to look out for your fallen brother. By this one good deed can cleanse every stain from your mouth. Why do I say cleanse? Because you will make your mouth as the mouth of God. And what honor could be equal to that? It is not I who make this promise to you. God himself said it. If you bring back one person, he said, your mouth will be cleansed and holy, as my mouth is.

(5) So let us not neglect our brothers, let us not go around saying: "How many kept the fast? How many were filched away from us?" Rather, let us show our concern for them. Even if those who observed the fast are many, you my beloved, must not make a show and a parade of this calamity in the Church; you must cure it. If someone tells you that many have observed the fast, stop him from talking so the rumor may not get around and become public knowledge. You say to him: "For my part, I don't know of anyone who observed it. You are mistaken, sir, and deceived. If you see two or three filched away, you say that these few are many." So stop this accuser from talking. But you must also see to it that you show your concern for those who *were* snatched away. Then you will keep the Church safe from a double hurt: first, by preventing the rumor from making the rounds and, secondly, by bringing back to the sacred fold the sheep who were snatched away.

(6) Therefore, let us not go around asking: "Who fell into sin?" Let our only zeal be to set straight those who have sinned. It is a dangerous practice and a terrible thing only to accuse your brothers and not to come to their aid, to parade in public the sins of the sick and not cure them. Let us, then get rid of this wicked practice, my beloved, for it leads to no small harm.

(7) Let me tell you how it does this. Somebody hears you say that there were many who observed the fast with the Jews and, without any

---

[11] Jer. 15:19

further investigation, he spreads the story to someone else. And the second man, without inquiring into the truth of the rumor, again tells it to still another. Then, as the evil rumor little by little grows greater, it spreads a great disgrace over the Church. And this does no good for those who have fallen away; in fact, it causes considerable harm both to them and to many others.

(8) Even if those who did fall are in number, we make them a multitude by the multitude of our rumors; we weaken those who resisted and we give a push to those on the point of falling. If one of our brothers hears the rumor that a large number joined in keeping the Jewish fast, he will be more inclined to be careless himself; again, if it is one of weak ones who hears the story, he will rush to join the strong of those who have fallen. Even if many have sinned, let us not join with those who rejoice at this or any other evil. If we do, we make a parade of the sinners and say that their name is legion. Rather, let us stop the rumormongers and keep them from spreading the story.

(9) Do not tell me that those who observed the fast are many. Even if they are many, you must set them straight. I did not expend all these words for you to accuse many, but for you to make the many few, and to save even these few. Therefore, do not put their sins on parade, but treat their wounds. Some people parade rumors and have time only for that. They see to it that the number of those who have sinned is judged to be large even if only a few have fallen. In the same way, if people reprove the rumormongers and shut their mouths, if they show concern for those who have fallen, no matter how many they be, it is no hard task for them to set the sinner straight. And furthermore, they keep those rumors from doing harm to anyone else.

(10) You have heard David's lament for Saul when he said: "How are the mighty fallen! Tell it not in Gath, publish it not in the streets of Ashkelon; lest the daughters of the Philistines rejoice, lest the daughters of the uncircumcised exult".[12] If David did not wish the matter paraded in public so that it might not be a source of joy to his foes, so much the more must we avoid spreading the story to alien ears. Rather, we must not spread it even among ourselves for fear that our enemies may hear it and rejoice, for fear that our own may learn of it and fall. We must hush

---

[12] 2 Sam. 1:19-20

it up and keep it guarded on every side. Do not say to me, "I told so-and-so." Keep the story to yourself. If you did not manage to keep quiet, neither will he manage to keep his tongue from wagging.

V

(1) What I say applies not only to the actual observance of the fast but also to ten thousand other sins. Let us not only ask if many were filched away; let us ask how we may bring them back. Let us not exalt our enemies' side and destroy our own. Let us not show that they are strong and that our side is weak. Let us do quite the opposite. Rumor can often destroy a soul but, just as often, it can lift it up; it can put zeal in a soul where was none and, again, it can destroy the zeal that was there.

(2) So I urge you to increase the rumors which exalt our cause and show its greatness, but not the rumors which spread shame on the community of our brothers. If we hear something good, let us broadcast it to all; if we hear something bad or evil, let us keep that hidden among ourselves and do everything we can to get rid of the evil. Therefore, let us now go forth, let us get busy and search for the sinner, let us not shrink back even if we must go into his home. If you do not know him, if you have no connection with him, get busy and find some friend or relative of his, someone to whom he pays particular attention. Take this man with you and go into his home.

(3) Do not blush or feel ashamed. If you were going there to ask for money or to get some favor from him, you have reason to feeling ashamed. If you hurry to save the man, no one can find fault with your motive for entering his home. Sit down and talk with him. But start your conversation on other topics so that he does not suspect that the real purpose of your visit is to set him straight.

(4) Say to him: "Tell me, do you approve of the Jews for crucifying Christ, for blaspheming him as they do, and for calling him a lawbreaker?" If the man is a Christian, he will never put up with this; even be he a Judaizer times without number, he will never bring himself to say: "I do approve." Rather, he will stop up his ears and say to you: "Heaven forbid! Be quiet, man." Next, after you find that he agrees with you, take the matter again and say: "How is it that you attend their services, how is it you participate in the festival, how is it you join them in observing the fast?" Then accuse the Jews of being obstinate. Tell him about their every

transgression which I recounted to your loving assembly in the days just past. Tell him of their transgressions connected with the place, the time and the temple, and how the prophets gave proof of these in their predictions. Show him how the whole ritual of the Jews is useless and unavailing. Show him that they will never return to their old commonwealth and way of life and that they are forbidden to fulfill, except in Jerusalem, what the old life demanded.

(5) Furthermore, remind him of Gehenna. Remind him of the test he will undergo before the Lord's dread tribunal of judgment. Remind him that we will give an accounting for all these things and that no small punishment awaits those who dare to do what he is doing. Remind him that Paul said: "You who would be justified by the law; you have fallen away from grace".[13] Remind him of Paul's threat: "Now I, Paul, say to you that if you receive circumcision, Christ will be of no advantage to you".[14] Tell him that, as is the case with circumcision, so, too, the fasting of the Jews drives from heaven the man who observes the fast, even if he has ten thousand other good works to his credit. Tell him that we have the name of Christians because we believe in Christ and not because we run to those who are His foes.

(6) Suppose he uses the cures which the Jews effect as his excuse; suppose he says: *"They promise to make me well, and so I go to them."* Then you must reveal the tricks they use, their incantations, their amulets, their charms and spells. This is the only way in which they have a reputation for healing; they do not effect genuine cures. Heaven forbid they should! Let me go so far as to say that even if they really do cure you, it is better to die than to run to God's enemies and be cured that way. What use is it to have your body cured if you lose your soul? What profit is there that you find some relief from your pain in this world if you are going to be consigned to eternal fire?

(7) So that no Jew may say that he will cure you, listen to what God said: "If a prophet arises among you, or a dreamer of dreams, and gives you a sign or a wonder, and the sign or wonder which he tells you comes to pass, and if he says, 'Let us go after other gods,' which you have not known, 'and let us serve them,' you shall not listen to the words of that

---

[13] Gal. 5:4
[14] Gal. 5:2

prophet or that dreamer of dreams; for the Lord your God is testing you, to know whether you love the Lord your God with all your heart and with all your soul".[15]

(8) What God means is this. Suppose some prophet says to you: "I can raise a dead man to life or cure a blind man. But you must obey me when I say: 'Let us worship demons, or let us offer sacrifice to idols'." Then, suppose the man who said this *can* cure a blind man or raise a dead man to life. God said that you must not heed him because of these signs and wonders which he works. Why? Because God is testing you, he permitted that man to have this power. It is not that God does not know your thoughts but that he is giving you a chance to prove if you really love him. And there are men who are eager to drag us away from our Beloved. Even if they show dead men brought back to life, the man who truly loves God will not stand apart from God because he has seen such signs and wonders.

(9) If God said this to the Jews, he says it all the more to us. We are the ones he led to a greater life of virtue. He opened the door for us to rise again. He gave the command to us not to love our dwelling here on earth but to keep all our hopes aimed at the life to come.

VI

(1) But what are you saying? Is it that a bodily ailment is afflicting you and crushing you? You have not suffered as many ills as did blessed Job. You have not endured even the slightest part of his pain. First, he lost the whole throng of his flocks, his herds, and every other possession. Then the whole chorus of his children was snatched off. And all this happened on a single day, so that not only the nature of his calamities but also the unbroken succession of his losses might crush this athlete down to earth.

(2) After all that, he received a lethal blow on his body, he saw worms swarming forth from his flesh, he sat naked on a dung hill, a public spectacle of disaster for all men there to see, Job the just, truthful, God-fearing man who kept himself aloof from every evil deed. And his troubles did not stop there. All day, all night, he suffered distress, and a strange and unusual hunger assailed him. He said: "My appetite refuses

---

[15] Deut. 13:1-3

to touch them; they are as food that is loathsome to me".[16] Each day he was reproached, scoffed at, mocked, and ridiculed. He said: "Then you scare me with dreams and terrify me with visions",[17] "My breath is strange to my wife, and I am a stench to the children of my own mother".[18] "Terrors are turned upon me; my honor is pursued as by the wind, and my prosperity has passed away like a cloud".[19]

(3) But his wife promised him freedom from all these things when she said: "Curse God, and die".[20] What she meant was: "Curse God and you will be free from the troubles which oppress you." Did her advice change the mind of that holy man? It did just the opposite; it gave him great strength so that he even reproached his wife. He chose to feel pain, to endure hardship, and to suffer ten thousand terrible things rather than curse God and so find release from his terrible troubles.

(4) The man who had been 38 years in the grip of his infirmity used to rush each year to the pool and each year he was driven back and found no cure. Each year he would see others cured because they had many to take of them. But he had no one to put him in the water ahead of the others and so remained in the constant grip of his paralysis. Even so, he did not run to the soothsayers, he did not go to the charm-users, he did not tie an amulet around his neck, but he waited for God to help him. That is why he finally found a wonderful and unexpected cure.

(5) Lazarus wrestled all his days with hunger, disease, and poverty, not only for 38 years but for his whole life. At any rate, he died while he was lying at the gateway of the rich man, scorned, scoffed at, famished, laid out before the dogs for food. For his body had grown to weak to scare away the dogs who came and licked his wounds. Yet he did not search for a soothsayer, he did not tie tokens around his neck, and he did not resort to the charm-users, he did not call in those skilled in witchcraft, nor did he do anything he was forbidden to do. He chose to die from these troubles of his rather than betray, in any small way, his life of godliness.

(6) Look at the torments and sufferings those men endured! What excuse will we have if, for our fevers and hurts, we run to the synagogues,

---

[16] Job 6:7
[17] Job 7:14
[18] Job 19:17
[19] Job 30:15
[20] Job 2:9

if we summon into our own house these sorcerers, these dealers in witch-craft? Hear what the Scripture says: "My son, if you come forward to serve the Lord, prepare yourself for temptation. Set your heart right and be stead-fast, and do not be hasty in time of calamity. Hold to him and do not de-part, that you may be honored at the end of your life. Accept whatever is brought upon you, and in changes that humble you be patient. For gold is tested in the fire, and acceptable men in the furnace of humiliation".[21]

(7) Suppose you flog your servant. Suppose, that, after you have dealt him 30 or 50 lashes, he then loudly demands his freedom, or that he flees from your control to take refuge with men who hate you. Suppose that he then incites them against you. Tell me this. Can he get you to for-give him? Can anyone offer a defense in his behalf? Of course not.

(8) But why? Because it is a master's duty to punish his servant. And this is not the only reason. If the slave had to run away, he should not have gone to the enemies who hated his master; he should have gone to his master's true friends. You must do the same. When you see that God is punishing you, do not flee to his enemies, the Jews, so that you may not rouse his anger against you still further. Run instead to martyrs, to the saints, to those in whom he is well pleased and who can speak to him with great confidence and freedom.

(9) But why talk about slaves and masters? If a father flogs his son, the son cannot do what the slave did, nor can he deny his relationship to his father. Suppose the father flogs his son, suppose he keeps him from his table, suppose he drives him from his house, and punishes him every way he can. Both the laws of nature and those established by man com-mand the son to be brave and endure all this. No one ever excuses the son if he refuses to obey his father and put up with the punishment. Even if the boy who was flogged lifts his voice in ten thousand bitter laments, everyone will tell him that it was his father who flogged him, that his father is the master and the power to do whatever he wants, that the son must meekly endure it all.

(10) So, then, slaves put up with their masters and sons put up with their fathers even though the punishments they get often do not fit the fault. Will you refuse to put up with God when He corrects you? Is he not more your master than your master is? Does he not love you more

---

[21] Sirach 2:1-5

than any father? When he interferes and does something, it is not done from anger. He does everything for your own good. If you get some slight illness, will you reject him as your master and rush off to the demons and desert over to the synagogues? What pardon will you find after that? How can you call on Him for help again? Who else will be able to plead your cause even if he could speak with the freedom and confidence of a Moses? There is no one.

(11) Do you not hear what God said to Jeremiah about the Jews? "Though Moses and Samuel stood before me, yet my heart would not turn toward this people".[22] That is how far some sins go beyond forgiveness and how incapable of defense they are. Therefore, let us not draw down such anger on ourselves. Even if the Jews seem to relieve your fever with their incantations, they are not relieving it. They are bringing down on your conscience another more dangerous fever. Every day you will feel the sting of remorse; every day your conscience will flog you. And what will your conscience say? "You sinned against God, you transgressed his Law, you violated your covenant with Christ. For an insignificant ailment you betrayed your faith. You are not the only one who has suffered this ailment, are you? Have not others been much more seriously ill that you? Still no one of them dared commit such a sin. But you were so soft and weak that you sacrificed your soul. What defense will you make to Christ? How will you ask for his help in your prayers? With what conscience will you set foot in the church? With what eyes will you look at the priest? With what hands will you touch the sacred banquet? With what ears will you listen to the reading of the scriptures there?"

VII

(1) Every day your reason will sting you and your conscience will flog you with these words. What kind of health is this when we have such thoughts in our minds to accuse us? But if you put up with your fever for a little while, if you scorn those who want to chant over you an incantation or tie an amulet to your body, if you insult them roundly and drive them from your house, your conscience will immediately bring you relief like a drink of water. Even if the fever recurs time and time again, even if

---

[22] Jer. 15:1

it is burning up your body, your soul brings you a solace that is better and more profitable than any relief from water or perspiration.

(2) Even if you recover your health after the incantation, the thought of the sin you committed leaves you worse off than those who are tossed with fever. And if you are the one who has the fever now, if you are the one who suffers ten thousand torments, you will be better off than any healthy man, because you have gotten rid of those foul sorcerers. Your reason will exult, your soul will rejoice and be glad, your conscience will praise you and voice its approval.

(3) And what will your conscience say? "Well done, well done, good man. You are the servant of Christ, you are the man of faith, the athlete of the godly life. You chose to die in torment rather than betray the life of godliness entrusted to your care. You will stand with the martyrs on that day. The martyrs chose to be flogged and torn on the rack that God might hold them in honor. So you chose this day to be flogged and racked with fever and wounds rather than submit to profane incantations and amulets. Because you nurture yourself with these hopes, you will not feel the torments which assail you".

(4) If this fever does not carry you off, another one surely will; if we do not die now, we are sure to die later. It is our lot to have a body doomed to die. But we do not have this body so that we may heed its passions and take to ourselves a life of godlessness, but that we may use its passions for the godly life. If we live the sober life, this corruption, this same mortal body will become the basis for our honor and will give us great confidence not only on that day but also in the present life.

(5) So, go ahead and insult those sorcerers roundly and drive them from your house. Everybody who hears of it will praise you and marvel at you. People will say one to the other: "So-and-so was sick and in pain. Time and time again, people came to him and urged him, and advised him to subject himself to magic incantations. He did not give in, but said: "It is better to die the way I am than to betray my faith and the godly life." Those who hear these words will applaud him long and loud; they will be astounded and give glory to God.

(6) Do you not think this will be richer in honor than many statues, more brilliant in its magnificence than many portraits, more remarkable in its distinction than many dignities? Everyone will praise you, everyone will count you happy, everyone will crown you with the victor's wreath.

And they will be better themselves, they will experience a return to zeal, they will imitate your courage. If somebody else does what you did, you will carry off the reward because it was you who gave him his start; it is you whom he emulates.

(7) Your good deeds will not only bring praise to you but also rapid release from your sickness. The nobility of your choice will win God to even greater good will; all the saints will rejoice at what you have done; they will pray for you from the bottom of their hearts. If such courage brings these rewards in this life, consider what reward you will receive in heaven. In the presence of all the angels and archangels, Christ will come forward, take you by the hand, and lead you to the middle of that stage. Everyone will listen when he says:

(8) "This man was once gripped by fever. Many people urged him to be rid of his ailment, but, for my name's sake and because he feared he might offend me in some way, he scorned these people and thrust aside those who were promising to cure him in that fashion. He chose to die of his illness rather than betray his love for me."

(9) If Christ leads to the center of this stage those who gave him to drink, who clothed and fed him, he will do this all the more for those who endured fevers for his sake. Giving food and clothing is not the same thing as submitting to a long-continuing disease. To submit to the disease is a much greater thing. And the greater the suffering, the more glorious will be the reward.

(10) In sickness and in health, let us rehearse for this day and talk about it, one to the other. If we find ourselves in the grip of a fever we cannot endure, let us say to ourselves: "What about this? If someone brought a charge against me and I was dragged into court, if I were tied to the whipping post and my sides were torn with lashes, would I not have to put up with it at any rate, even though I would get no profit or reward?"

(11) Now let us ponder on this. Suppose there is set before you a reward for your patience and endurance; suppose the reward is large enough to encourage your fallen spirit. "But my fever is severe," you say, "and hard to bear." Then compare your fever to the fire of Gehenna. You will surely escape that fire if you show great endurance in putting up with your fever.

(12) Remember how many sufferings the apostles endured. Remember that the just were constantly afflicted. Remember that blessed Timothy had not rest from his illness, but lived with his disease from one end of his life to the other. Paul made this clear when he said: "Use a little wine for the sake of your stomach and your frequent ailments".[23] That just and holy man took in hand the superintendence of the world, brought the dead back to life, drove out demons, and cured ten thousand ailments in others. If he experienced such terrible suffering, what defense will you have for groaning and grieving over ailments which will last only for a time?

(13) Did you not listen to the Scripture? It says: "For the Lord disciplines him whom he loves, and chastises every son whom he receives".[24] How many times and how many men have yearned to receive the crown of martyrdom? In this, you have a perfect martyr's crown. A martyr is made not only when someone is ordered to offer sacrifices to die rather than offer the sacrifice. If a man shuns any practice, and to shun it can only bring on death, he is certainly a martyr.

VIII

(1) So that you may know that this is true, remember how John (the Baptist) died, from what motive and why. Remember, too, how Abel died. Neither John nor Abel saw an altar with its fire, nor a statue standing before them. They heard no voice commanding them to offer sacrifice. John only reproached Herod and had his head cut off; Abel merely honored God with a more excellent sacrifice than his brother did, and Cain slew him. They were not deprived of martyr's crowns, were they? Who would dare to say that? The very way they died is enough to make everyone agree that they belong in the front ranks of the martyrs.

(2) If you are looking for some divine proclamation about these two men, listen to what Paul said. He made it clear that his words are the words of the Holy Spirit when he said: "I think that I have the Spirit of God".[25] What then, did Paul say? He began with Abel and told how Abel offered to God a more excellent sacrifice than Cain, and through his faith, through he is dead, he yet speaks.

---

[23] 1 Tim. 5:23
[24] Heb. 12:6
[25] 1 Cor. 7:40

(3) Then Paul continued his account down through the prophets and came to John. After he said: "They were stoned, they were sawn in two, they were killed with the sword";[26] after he recounted many and different modes of martyrdom, he went on to say: "Therefore, since we are surrounded by so great a cloud of witnesses, let us also lay aside every weight, and sin which clings so closely, and let us run with perseverance the race that is set before us".[27] Do you see that he also called Abel a martyr, along with Noah, Abraham, Isaac, and Jacob? For some of these died for God's sake in the same way that Paul spoke of, when he said: "I die every day";[28] they died not by dying but only by their willingness to endure death.

(4) If you do this, if you reject the incantations, the spells, and the charms, and if you then die of your disease, you will be a perfect martyr. Even though others promised your relief along with an ungodly life, you chose death with godliness. And I have spoken these words to those boastful talkers who say that the demons do effect cures. To learn how false this is, listen to what Christ said about the devil: "He was a murderer from the beginning".[29] God says he is a murderer; do you rush to him as you would to a physician?

(5) Tell me this. When you stand indicted before God's tribunal, what reason will you be able for considering the Jews' witchcraft more worthy of your belief than what Christ has said? God said that the devil is a murderer; they say that he can cure diseases, in contradiction to God's word. When you accept their charms and incantations, your actions show that you consider the Jews more worthy of your belief than God, even if you do not say it in so many words.

(6) If the devil is a murderer, it is clear that the demons who serve him are murderers, too. What Christ did has taught you this lesson. At any rate, he gave the demons leave to enter into the herd of swine and the demons drove the whole herd down the cliff and drowned them. He did this so that you might know that the demons would have done the same thing to human beings and would have drowned them if God had allowed them to do so. But he restrained the demons, stopped them, and

---

[26] Heb. 11:37
[27] Heb. 12:1
[28] 1 Cor. 15:31
[29] John 8:44

permitted them to do no such thing. Once they had gotten power over the swine, the demons made quite clear what they would have done to us. If they did not spare the swine, it is all the more sure they would not have kept their hands off us. Therefore, beloved, do not be swept off by the deceits of the demons but stand firm in your fear of God.

(7) But how will you go into the synagogue? If you make the sign of the cross on your forehead, the evil power that dwells in the synagogue immediately takes to flight. If you fail to sign your forehead, you have immediately thrown away your weapon at the doors. Then the devil will lay hold of you, naked and unarmed as you are, and he will overwhelm you with ten thousand terrible wounds.

(8) What need is there for me to say this? The way you act when you get to the synagogue makes it clear that you consider it a very serious sin to go to that wicked place. You are anxious that no one notice your arrival there; you urge your household, friends, and neighbors not to report you to the priests. If someone does report you, you fly into a rage. Would it not be the height of folly to try to hide from men your bold and shameless when God, who is present everywhere, sees it?

(9) Are you not afraid of God? Then, at least, stand in some awe and fear of the Jews. How will you look them in the eye? How will you speak to them? You profess you are a Christian, but you rush off to their synagogues and beg them to help you. Do not realize how they laugh at you, scoff at you, jeer at you, dishonor you, and reproach you? Even if they do not do it openly, do you not understand that they are doing this deep down in their hearts?

IX

(1) Tell me, then. Will you put up with the taunts of the Jews? Will you tolerate them? Suppose you had to suffer incurable ills; suppose you had to die ten thousand deaths. Would it not be much better to endure all that rather than have those abominable people laugh and scoff at you, rather than live with a bad conscience?

(2) My purpose in speaking is not to have you hear this for yourselves; I want you also to work to cure those who have this sickness. They are feeble in their faith, and for this I blame them. I also blame you for your unwillingness to set the sick ones straight. It is not in question that, when you come here to the church, you listen to what is said; you

leave yourself open to condemnation when you fail to follow through with action the words you hear.

(3) Why are you a Christian? Is it not that you may imitate Christ and obey his Laws? What did Christ do? He did not sit in Jerusalem and call the sick to come to him. He went around to cities and towns and cured sickness of both body and soul. He could have stayed sitting in the same place and still have drawn all men to himself. But he did not do this. Why? So that he might give us the example of going around in search of those who are perishing.

(4) He gave us another glimpse of this example in the parable of the shepherd.[30] The shepherd did not sit down with the 99 sheep and wait for the lost one to come to him. He went out himself and found it. And after he found the lost sheep, he lifted it to his shoulders and brought it back. Do you not see that a physician does this same thing? He does not force patients who are confined to bed to be brought to his home. The physician himself hurries to the homes of the sick.

(5) You must do this, too, beloved. You know that the present life is short; if we do not earn our profits here, we will have no salvation hereafter. Gaining a single soul can often erase the burden of countless sins and be the price which buys us life on that day. Ponder on this question. Why were we sent prophets, apostles, just men, and often even angels? Why did the only-begotten Son of God come among us himself? Was it not to save men? Was it not to bring back those who had strayed?

(6) You must do this with all the strength you have. You must devote all your zeal and concern to bringing back those who have strayed. At every religious service, let me keep exhorting you to do this; whether you pay attention or not, I will not stop saying it. Whether you listen or not, it is God's law that I fulfill this ministry. If you listen to me and do what I say, I will keep on doing this and feel great joy. If you disregard it and become indifferent to what I say, I will keep on saying it but with great fear instead of joy.

(7) If you disobey, it will involve no risk for me hereafter. I have fulfilled my part. Even if there will be no danger for me because I have carried out my full fair share, I will feel sorrow for you when you are

---

[30] Matt. 18:12-14; Luke 15:3-7

accused on that day. Even listening to me will be fraught with danger, when you fail to follow up my words with your deeds.

(8) Hear, at any rate, how Christ both reproved the teachers who buried the meaning of his message but how he also terrified those whom they taught. For after he said: "Then you ought to have invested my money with the bankers," he went on to add: "And on my return I should have demanded it back with interest".[31]

(9) What Christ showed by the parable was this. After hearing a sermon (for this is depositing the money), those who have received the instruction must make it produce interest. The interest from the teaching is nothing other than proving through deeds what you have been taught through words. Since I have deposited my money in your ears, you must now pay your teacher back the interest, that is, you must save your brothers. So, if you should just keep holding on to what I said and produce no interest by action on your own part, I am afraid that you will pay the same penalty as the servant who buried his coins in the ground. And for this he was bound hand and foot and cast into the darkness outside, because the words he heard brought no profit to others.

(10) So that we may not have this happen to us, let us imitate the servant who received five coins and not the one who received two. Whatever you will be asked to spend to save your neighbor, be it words, money, bodily pain, or anything else whatsoever, we must not shrink back or hesitate. Then each of us, in every way, will multiply proportionately the talent given him by God. Then each of us will be able to hear those happy words: "Well done, good and faithful servant; you have been faithful over a little, I will set you over much; enter into the joy of your master".[32] May we all gain this by the grace and loving-kindness of our Lord Jesus Christ through whom and with whom be glory and power to the Father together with the Holy Spirit, world without end. Amen.

---

[31] Matt. 25:27
[32] Matt. 25:21

APPENDIX
SUPPLEMENTAL TEXT TO HOMILY II

The Law did help our nature very much—but only if it genuinely leads us to Christ; by the same token, if it does not do this, it has actually hurt us, by depriving us of greater things through attention to smaller things, and by continuing to keep us confined in the countless wounds of our transgressions. Indeed, suppose there were two doctors, the one less powerful and the other more powerful; and the one, although he applied medicines to the patient's sores, was not able to free the afflicted person once and for all from the pain they caused, but only brought some slight relief, whereas when the other doctor, the more powerful one, arrived, taking all those medicines away and simply washing the sick person, he was able to purify him of his afflictions, leaving no further trace—not even the slightest mark. And then, suppose that the first doctor tried to prevent the patient from being treated by that [better doctor]. What help could he possibly provide by the application of his medicines, that would be as great as the damage he caused by preventing the patient from taking the brief way, the quickest way to health?

This is also how you should think, when it comes to Christ and the Law. The Law applies medicines, bringing altogether slight relief for our sores. Christ, on the other hand, when he came, took away all these things and by washing us with the water of baptism, he allowed no trace or mark of our previous wounds to remain. So then, one who still clings to the Law is doing nothing but disbelieving in the skill of the doctor, and denying that baptism is sufficient to take away his trespasses. For running to the law is the mark of one who is afraid that Christ is not strong enough to free us from our prior sins through his own grace—and this is proof of the worst unbelief: such people are committing outrage on both the Law and on Christ, disbelieving both the one and the other. By clinging to the Law, they are disbelieving in Christ's grace; but by clinging to it only in part, they have charged it with great weakness.

Tell me: Is the law alone, by itself, able to justify? [Yes?] Well then, why do you not fulfill it completely? But it is fairly weak and feeble—

Obviously you think so, if you only keep it in part! Again, is Christ able to grant the forgiveness of all your sins? [Yes?] Well then, why do you cling to the Law, and fear that you will be judged as a transgressor for not keeping one of the Law's commandments? This is the mark of those who do not truly have confidence in Christ's kindness. At this point, it is timely to say, "Woe to timid hearts and to slack hands, and to the sinner who walks along two ways!"[1] For you must imagine that what has been said about circumcision has also been said about fasting, and about every other commandment of the Law, if you keep it now, at the wrong time— just as, if someone is now circumcised, "Christ will be of no benefit" to him. Indeed, so that you will not think this statement only pertained to circumcision, but instead [understand that it applied] to the entire Law, if someone were to keep it now, at the wrong time, you must listen to what he says: "You who would be justified by the law; you have fallen away from grace".[2] What further punishment could there be to equal this one? But may this not happen to our brothers! I do call them brothers, even if they are sick in countless ways, because of my hopes for their health.

Now then, let me strip down for the fight against the Jews them-selves, so that the victory may be more glorious—so that you will learn that they are abominable and lawless and murderous and enemies of God. For there is no evidence of wickedness I can proclaim that is equal to this. But, in order to amass forensic-style speeches against them, I shall first demonstrate that even if they had not been deprived of their ancestral way of life, even so their fast would be polluted and impure— and I shall provide the proofs from the Law itself, and from Moses. For if it was lawless when it was observed while the Law was in effect and in power, so much the more now that the Law has ceased. And I shall demonstrate that not only the fast, but also all the other practices which they observe—sacrifices and purifications and festivals—are all abomi-nable. And when the very manner of purification is illegal as practiced, and would be rejected as loathsome, which of their other [rituals] can purify them thereafter?

The best starting point for the demonstration will be their ob-servance with regard to the place. For God led them out of the whole

---

[1] Ecclus. 2:12
[2] Gal. 5:4

world and confined them in a single place, Jerusalem. And in no other place were they permitted to fast, to sacrifice, to celebrate festivals or tabernacles, or indeed to read the Law, at the time when the Law was in force. And if back then, whenever these rites were conducted outside Jerusalem, the procedure constituted transgression, all the more so now. If you wish, I will read the laws that were set down for them concerning these matters. First, let me recite the law set down concerning the festival of Passover: "You may not offer the Passover sacrifice within any of your towns which the Lord your God gives you; but at the place which the Lord your God will choose, to make his name dwell in it".[3]— meaning Jerusalem (for his name had been called over that city, as Daniel also made plain when he prayed and said, "Open thy eyes and behold our desolations, and the city which is called by thy name".[4] He used this term for the city not because God has a city—of course not!—but in order to make the place more awesome by virtue of the fear inherent in the appellation.

So then, this law is one that prohibits them from carrying out the sacrifices of the Passover [anywhere outside Jerusalem], not only in Syria and Cilicia and among other peoples, but even in Palestine itself. "For you shall not be able to celebrate the Passover in any of the cities which the Lord your God gives you"—and the cities he gave were in Judaea. Do you see how they have been forced out, not out of the world, but out of the [rest of the] province itself, into one single place? Again, concerning the festival which is now imminent, he warns, "You shall keep the feast of booths seven days, when you make your ingathering from your threshing floor and your wine press".[5] For because they were ungrateful and unmindful of their benefactor, he bound their remembrances of the kindness of God into the necessities of their festivals.

And at the same time, they would learn the reason for the festival: For when the harvest is complete, he says, celebrate days of thanksgiving to the giver of the requested sustenance—"You shall rejoice in your feast, you and your son and your daughter, your manservant and your maidservant, the Levite, the sojourner, the fatherless, and the widow who are within your towns. For seven days you shall keep the feast to

---

[3] Deut. 16:5-6
[4] Dan. 9:18
[5] Deut. 16:13

the Lord your God at the place which the Lord will choose".[6] And as for the fact that they were not even allowed to read the Law outside Jerusalem, listen to this: "At the end of every seven years, at the set time of the year of release, at the feast of booths, when all Israel comes to appear before the Lord your God at the place which he will choose, you shall read this law before all Israel in their hearing";[7] there you shall fast for the Feast of Tabernacles. Do you see that he preserves this [stipulation] also in the case of the fast?

Next, in order not to go through each thing individually, he added in summary fashion that it was in no way permitted for them to carry out their customary rituals of worship anywhere else, saying, "Take heed that you do not offer your burnt offerings at every place that you see; but at the place which the Lord will choose in one of your tribes, there you shall offer your burnt offerings, and there you shall do all that I am commanding you".[8] For when he said "all," he included, by using this word, festivals and sacrifices and lustrations and purifications and whatever else was in the Law. Then, because they were thoughtless and senseless, and his exhortation was not sufficient to persuade them, he also added an inexorable punishment for those who disobeyed: "And the Lord said to Moses, 'Say to Aaron and his sons and to all the people of Israel, this is the thing which the Lord has commanded. If any man of the house of Israel kills an ox or a lamb or a goat in the camp, or kills it outside the camp, and does not bring it to the door of the tent of meeting, to offer it as a gift to the Lord before the tabernacle of the Lord, bloodguilt shall be imputed to that man; he has shed blood."[9]

What does it mean that "blood shall be reckoned for him"? He will be condemned for murder, having become just like a murderer—for [God] was not paying attention to the nature of what was sacrificed, but to the mindset of the one who was sacrificing. For this reason, it was reckoned as murder: because the slaughter took place contrary to God's wishes. Do you see how closely guarded the [issue of] place was? The one who does not sacrifice at the doors of the Tent of Witness, he says, will be punished just as if he has killed a human being, even if he is sacri-

---

[6] Deut. 16:14-15
[7] Deut. 31:10-11
[8] Deut. 12:13
[9] Lev. 17:1-4

ficing a sheep. And further tightening the punishment, he says, "And that man shall be cut off from among his people".[10] Why? Because he did not bring his sacrifices to the doors of the Tent of Witness, he then says. And why does he order them to sacrifice there? So that they will not sacrifice to their idols and "for goat demons, after whom they play the harlot".[11]

Do you see that the very reason is an indictment of their impiety and prostitution? (For he always calls their impiety prostitution.) He drove them together from all quarters into a single place for this reason: so that they would have no occasion for impiety. When a well-born and free man has a female slave who is licentious and pulls in all the passers-by for immoral relations with her, he does not allow her to go out into the neighborhood, to show herself in the alley-way, to rush into the market-place; instead, he confines her upstairs in the house, shackles her with iron, and orders her to remain indoors at all times, so that both the spatial restrictions of the place and the compulsion of the chains will be her starting-point for chastity. God acted in the very same way: the Synagogue being his licentious slave-woman, gaping after every demon and every idol, and rushing to make sacrifices to the idols in every spot and in every place, he confined it in Jerusalem and the temple, as though in the master's house, and ordered it to sacrifice and celebrate festivals at appointed times there only, so that both the spatial restrictions of the place and the observance of the times would keep it, even unwillingly, in the law of piety. Sit there and be modest, he says; let the place train you, since your character did not.

And [to confirm] that this is the reason why he commanded sacrifice there only: you have heard the Law that has now been read among us—it runs as follows: "That they may bring them to the Lord, to the priest at the door of the tent of meeting"[12]—and it goes on to add the reason: "So they shall no more offer their sacrifices for goat demons, after whom they play the harlot".[13] For there was no spot in Palestine that was not defiled by their impiety; instead, every hill, every ravine, and every tree was privy to this impiety of theirs. For this reason, Hosea cried out and said, "They sacrifice on the tops of the mountains, and make offer-

---

[10] Lev. 17:4
[11] Lev. 17:7
[12] Lev. 17:5
[13] Lev. 17:7

ings upon the hills, under oak, poplar, and terebinth, because their shade is good".[14] And Jeremiah said, "Lift up your eyes to the bare heights, and see! Where have you not been lain with?"[15] It was for this reason that God, seeing that they had gone astray, confined them in one spot: the temple.

But not even this put a stop to their licentiousness; rather, as if obstinately wishing to demonstrate to their Lord that whatever he did they would not abandon their madness, they brought adulterous lovers into their Lord's house, at one time setting up a four-faced idol there, at another time painting the abominations of reptiles and cattle on the wall. Ezekiel made this known to us—for he was brought from Babylon to the temple, and when he saw them burning incense to the sun and mourning for Adonis and worshipping all the other idols in the temple itself, he cried out in distress.

But the prophet did not point out only this rampant impiety, but also [approached the subject] in another way, speaking as follows: "So you were different from other women in your harlotries".[16] How is it that payments are made to all prostitutes, he says, "none solicited you to play the harlot; and you gave hire, while no hire was given to you"?[17] For they engaged in prostitution and paid money for their own prostitution, which is the greatest proof of a soul that is being driven mad by the sting of its own profligacy. So then, because the house did not make them modest—instead, they set up their idols there—in the end God razed the temple itself to the ground. For what need was there for that place, given that idols were standing there and demons were being served in it?

Now I want to reckon up just what I promised you at first. What was it, then, that I promised? To show that they are transgressing in all that they now do—and in the first place, in the festival of Passover. The fact that they are not simply transgressing the Law, but are manifestly also murderers, when they celebrate this festival outside Jerusalem, is clear from what I have said. This has been proved most abundantly, by the grace of God. Therefore, whenever they sacrifice the Passover [lamb] either here or elsewhere, they are manifestly murderers. For if, when

---

[14] Hosea 4:13
[15] Jer. 3:2
[16] Ezek. 16:34
[17] Ezek. 16:34

someone does not bring his sacrifice to the doors of the Tent of Witness, the sacrifice is reckoned as blood and murder, and if these people make their sacrifices not only outside the temple, but even outside the city, indeed everywhere on earth, then it is quite obvious that they are enmeshed in the pollution [of murder] to an enormous degree.

In the same way, when they celebrate the Feast of Tabernacles and their other festivals, they are again impure and defiled. For if everything is purified by means of the sacrifices, and "without the shedding of blood there is no forgiveness of sins",[18] then once all the sacrifices have been taken away with the destruction of the temple, it necessarily follows that the methods of purification and the customs of all the festivals have been taken away—or that if they are practiced, they cause even greater pollution because they are performed in an unlawful manner.

Not only were they not permitted to sacrifice outside the temple—they were not even permitted to sing elsewhere, as the prophet also made plain. For when they had been carried off to Babylon, and those who had taken them captive wanted to hear Jewish song, and would say to them, "Sing us one of the songs of Zion!"[19] they would answer, by way of informing them that it was not permissible to sing outside Jerusalem, "How shall we sing the Lord's song in a foreign land?"[20] But neither did they fast in a foreign land; listen to what God said to them through Zechariah: "When you fasted and mourned in the fifth month and in the seventh, for these seventy years, was it for me that you fasted?"[21]—referring indirectly to the time of the captivity. It has also been proved that they were permitted to make sacrifices there only. For this reason, the three children said, "And at this time there is no prince, or prophet, or leader...no place to make an offering before thee or to find mercy."

Now of course there was a place in Babylonia—but not the customary place. For they hearkened to Moses, who said, "Take heed that you do not offer your burnt offerings at every place that you see; but at the place which the Lord will choose".[22] Thus, when they were allowed neither to sacrifice nor to sing nor to be purified nor to read the Law (for

---

[18] Heb. 9:22
[19] Ps. 137:3
[20] Ps. 137:4
[21] Zech. 7:5
[22] Deut. 12:13-14

indeed, another prophet likewise made the same charge when he said—and brought it out as a great accusation—"They read the Law outside and invoked confession"—when, therefore, they were allowed to do none of these things, what defense will they possibly have hereafter? They condemn and defile themselves by their myriad paths of transgression. And that is why I called their fast impure right from the beginning: because it is carried out unlawfully. Indeed, their Passover and Feast of Tabernacles, and whatever else they do, are profane and abominable; what they carry out is not worship, but lawlessness and transgression and outrage committed on God.

You see, if they did not dare to do any of these things during their sojourning in a foreign land (as my discourse has proved), when they expected to recover their ancestral city and return to the temple, then they are obligated much more now to stay idle, to refrain from action, and not to carry out any of these things—now that there is no longer any hope that they will recover Jerusalem. For that city shall not rise up again in the future, nor will they return to their prior form of worship. It was to make this clear to them that God opened up the whole world to them, and made that spot alone inaccessible, and thus there are imperial laws keeping them away and not allowing them to set foot in the doorway of the city—that city is and will remain off-limits for them at all times.

But on the very day of their fast, I will demonstrate that it [i.e., Jerusalem] will not rise again—if you are present again with the same enthusiasm and I see this hall made just as magnificent as it is now with the multitude of the listeners. Today, on the other hand, it is necessary to tell you why God opened the entire world to them, but made that city alone inaccessible to them. Why, then, did he do this? He knew their obstinacy and shamelessness, their willfulness and disobedience; he knew that they would not easily choose to give up their former way of life, conducted with sacrifices and burnt offerings, and go toward the higher, more spiritual life of the Gospels.

What, then, did he do? After tying their worship of him to the necessity of sacrifices, he furthermore confined the sacrifices themselves to the temple, and after doing this, he made the place off-limits for them, so that, from the fact that they were not allowed to set foot in Jerusalem, they would become aware that it was now not permissible for them to sacrifice—and from the absence of sacrifice they would be taught not to cling to the rest of their forms of worship any longer, and would be able to see that it was no longer the proper time for that way of life, that instead, God was calling them to a different and greater philosophy. A loving mother who has a nursing child, but later is eager to wean him away from milk-nourishment and lead him toward other kinds of nourishment—when she sees that he is unwilling and resistant, and continues to seek her breast and insinuate himself into her maternal bosom, she smears gall or some other kind of very bitter juice around the very nipple of her breast, and thus compels him, unwilling as he is, to turn away from the source of milk in future.

In the very same way, God, wanting to lead them to more solid nourishment, but then seeing them constantly running back to Jerusalem and its way of life, walled off the city like a mother's nipple with bile and the bitterest juice—the fear of the Romans—and by means of imperial decrees he made it become off-limits for them. His intention was that because of the desolation and the soldiers' weapons, they would stand aloof from that homeland and little by little become accustomed to rejecting their desire for milk and slipping into a love and craving for solid nourishment. For even though emperors caused the desolation, they were moved by God to do so, and this is clear from [a comparison with] the previous periods, when not even the ruler of the whole [world] was strong enough to take the city, since God was favorable to them. The temple was destroyed for this reason: so that they would no longer look for God in a place, but look up toward the heavens. Sacrifices were taken away for this reason: so that they would be able to see the true sacrifice as well, which took away the sin of the world. But if they are not willing [to change], then God, for his part, has displayed to them his kindness, while they, having made themselves unworthy of his goodness, will bring inexorable punishment upon themselves.

But now, it is time to leave behind my discourse with them, and to direct my criticism against those who have gone off to hear the Trumpets. Indeed, I ought not to have considered them even worth taking into account at this point, since after so much exhortation and advice they still persisted in the same stupidity. But I do expect to correct their ways by this second exhortation, and to persuade them to condemn their own stupidity with regard to their earlier [behavior]; thus, I eagerly embark on these remarks directed at them. For indeed, I know that by the grace of

God, many of those who were accustomed to do these things have departed from their wicked custom; and if not all were persuaded, yet they shall be persuaded by all means. A body that is beginning to be healthy makes progress on a path so as to cast off all its illness and finally return to a state of pure health.

You ran to hear the Trumpets? Tell me—(I wish to have a conversation with them in their absence, as though they were present. For even so does the soul that is in pain converse with people as though they are present and listening, even if those it is attacking are not listening)—so then, you ran to hear the Trumpets? Tell me: With those murderers? With those charlatans? With those delirious and raving-mad Jews? Did you not listen to Christ, who said, "But I say to you that everyone who looks at a woman lustfully has already committed adultery with her in his heart"?[23] For just as a licentious gaze produces adultery, so also untimely hearing works impiety.

But you desire to hear a trumpet! Then listen to the trumpet of Paul, the spiritual trumpet blaring out from the heavens and saying, "Therefore take the whole armor of God, that you may be able to withstand in the evil day, and having done all, to stand. Stand therefore, having girded your loins with truth, and having put on the breastplate of righteousness, and having shod your feet with the equipment of the gospel of peace; besides all these, taking the shield of faith, with which you can quench all the flaming darts of the evil one. And take the helmet of salvation, and the sword of the Spirit".[24]

Do you see how a spiritual trumpet arms you and leads you out to the battle against the demons? Listen to the thunder of John, saying: "In the beginning was the Word, and the Word was with God, and the Word was God".[25] Wait for the trumpet that [will sound] from the heavens: "For the trumpet will sound, and the dead will be raised".[26] Those who hear this [earthly] trumpet will not hear that [heavenly] one—or rather, they will hear it, but to their own detriment. For participation in the Jewish festival will mean participation in their punishment. At that time, the

---

[23] Matt. 5:28
[24] Eph. 6:13-17
[25] John 1:1
[26] 1 Cor. 15:52

Jews "look on him whom they have pierced".[27] What, then, [will happen,] if you appear in company with them? Is it not abundantly clear what is left [as the implication]? I am afraid to say it, but I impart it to your consciousness. You sound the trumpet with them now—so you will mourn with them then. But may it never be that any of the children of the churches be found in the gathering-place of those murderous people—not now, not ever! And that is why I have said this now: so that these things no longer take place.

But not only to men do I address these comments, but also to the women, through their husbands. For indeed, I know that most of the crowd that is drawn to go there is composed of women. Now then, the blessed Paul says, "Husbands, love your wives";[28] and again, "Let the wife see that she respects her husband".[29] But I am seeing neither wives' fear nor husbands' love. For if the wife feared her husband, she would not have dared to go. If the husband loved his wife, he would never have allowed and tolerated her going. For what is worse than this outrage, I ask you? A free and believing woman goes out of the house and goes off to a synagogue? Does she know any other place at all, apart from the church and the time spent there? But if she were going off to a lover, would you not have stood up? Would you not have been inflamed? Would you not have posted guards on all sides? But as it is, you do not see her going off to commit adultery with a man, but going off to [be with] demons—and you allow this impiety? If she commits a transgression against you, you punish her; but if she commits outrage against her Lord, you overlook it? If she wantonly abuses your marriage, you are a harsh and inexorable judge; but if she tramples on the covenants with God, you are careless and slack? How can these [offenses] be worthy of forgiveness?

And yet, God does not act that way, but rather in the opposite way: When he himself is outraged, he overlooks it; when you are treated that way, he punishes. Do you wish to learn that he honors your affairs more than his own? "So if you are offering your gift at the altar, and there remember that your brother has something against you, leave your gift

---

[27] Zech. 12:10
[28] Eph. 5:25
[29] Eph. 5:33

there before the altar and go; first be reconciled to your brother, and then come and offer your gift".[30]

---

[30] Matt. 5:23-24

INDEX OF BIBLE PASSAGES

(Extended passages are cited only by the initial chapter/verse)

INDEX

www.ingramcontent.com/pod-product-compliance
Lightning Source LLC
Chambersburg PA
CBHW051150120626
46547CB00012B/1023